# THE ALTO PART

*A Play in Two Acts*

by
BARBARA GILSTRAP

SAMUEL FRENCH, INC.
45 WEST 25TH STREET    NEW YORK 10010
7623 SUNSET BOULEVARD HOLLYWOOD 90046
LONDON                           TORONTO

Copyright ©, 1983, 1987, by Barbara Gilstrap

## ALL RIGHTS RESERVED

*CAUTION: Professionals and amateurs are hereby warned that THE ALTO PART is subject to a royalty. It is fully protected under the copyright laws of the United States of America, the British Commonwealth, including Canada, and all other countries of the Copyright Union. All rights, including professional, amateur, motion pictures, recitation, lecturing, public reading, radio broadcasting, television, and the rights of translation into foreign languages are strictly reserved. In its present form the play is dedicated to the reading public only.*

*THE ALTO PART may be given stage presentation by amateurs upon payment of a royalty of Fifty Dollars for the first performance, and Twenty-Five Dollars for each additional performance, payable one week before the date when the play is given, to Samuel French, Inc., at 45 West 25th Street, New York, N.Y. 10010, or at 7623 Sunset Boulevard, Hollywood, CA. 90046, or to Samuel French (Canada), Ltd. 80 Richmond Street East, Toronto, Ontario, Canada M5C 1P1.*

*Royalty of the required amount must be paid whether the play is presented for charity or gain and whether or not admission is charged.*

*Stock royalty quoted on application to Samuel French, Inc.*

*For all other rights than those stipulated above, apply to Samuel French, Inc.*

*Particular emphasis is laid on the question of amateur or professional readings, permission and terms for which must be secured in writing from Samuel French, Inc.*

*Copying from this book in whole or in part is strictly forbidden by law, and the right of performance is not transferable.*

*Whenever the play is produced the following notice must appear on all programs, printing and advertising for the play: "Produced by special arrangement with Samuel French, Inc."*

*Due authorship credit must be given on all programs, printing and advertising for the play.*

---

**Anyone presenting the play shall not commit or authorize any act or omission by which the copyright of the play or the right to copyright same may be impaired.**

---

**No changes shall be made in the play for the purpose of your production unless authorized in writing.**

---

**The publication of this play does not imply that it is necessarily available for performance by amateurs or professionals. Amateurs and professionals considering a production are strongly advised in their own interests to apply to Samuel French, Inc., for consent before starting rehearsals, advertising, or booking a theatre or hall.**

---

**No part of this book may be reproduced, stored in a retrieval system, or transmitted in any form, by any means, including mechanical, electronic, photocopying, recording, or otherwise, without the prior written permission of the publisher.**

---

ISBN 0 573 63028 3     Printed in U.S.A.

## IMPORTANT BILLING AND CREDIT REQUIREMENTS

All producers of THE ALTO PART *must* give credit to the Author of the Play in all programs distributed in connection with performances of the Play and in all instances in which the title of the Play appears for purposes of advertising, publicizing or otherwise exploiting the Play and/or a production. The name of the Author *must* also appear on a separate line, in which no other name appears, immediately following the title, and must appear in size of type not less than fifty percent the size of the title type.

**WPA THEATRE PRESENTS**
KYLE RENICK—ARTISTIC DIRECTOR
# THE ALTO PART
**by Barbara Gilstrap**
Directed by Zina Jasper
Setting by Edward T. Gianfrancesco
Lighting by Craig Evans
Costumes by Don Newcomb
Sound by Michael Kartzmer

*Cast in order of appearance*

| | |
|---|---|
| Mrs. Florene King | Kit Flanagan |
| Wanda King | Marisa Morell |
| Miss Ola Belle Archer | Carole Monferdini |
| Mrs. Hattie Eaton | Elizabeth Council |
| Miss Ethyl Roberts | Jane Hoffman |
| Miss Althea Lockwood | Jennifer Walker |

| | |
|---|---|
| Production Stage Manager | Mary Fran Loftus |
| Musical Direction and Piano Arrangements | Guy Strobel |
| Lights | Jack Scott |
| Sound | Craig Palanker |
| Costumes | Constance Tyler |
| Props | Rachel Kaufman |
| Assistant to Costume Designer | Leslie Meeker |
| Master Carpenter | Jeff Berzon |
| Graphics | Karen Florek |
| Typesetting | Straight Copy Composition |
| Photography | Ken Howard |

**The WPA Theatre extends a special thank you to:**
Susan Kennedy, Eagle Regalia Co., Inc.,
Manhattan Theatre Club, Equity Library Theatre, Broadway Clothing,
Michael-Jon Costumes, The Costume Collection, Theresa Quinn,
and the Association of Theatre Artists. Some props courtesy of
Joseph Papp and the New York Shakespeare Festival.

*All actors appear under the aegis of an Actors Equity Association Letter of Agreement*

The WPA Theatre is a member of the Alliance of Resident Theatres/New York

**First Performance: October 20, 1983**

---

This production is made possible with public funds from the
New York State Council on the Arts and the National Endowment for the Arts,
and by revenues earned from the commercial transfer
of the WPA production of *Little Shop of Horrors.*

## TIME

1956

## PLACE

Sparta, a small town in East Texas.

## SETTING

A wood frame duplex, which is noticeably without a foundation. It is perched precariously a foot or so off the ground on building blocks.

There are three playing areas—the Kings' side of the house, Hattie's side of the house, and the front porch. Entrances from and exits to the outside are made from the USR side of the porch.

The Kings occupy the SL side of the duplex. We see their living room, which also serves as Wanda's bedroom. At SC is a sofa with a coffee table in front of it. SR of the sofa is an end table with a lamp, and next to that is a chair. US of the sofa is a large, standing radio. At extreme SL is a dresser, over which is a mirror. On the same wall as the dresser and US of it is a closet. USL is a curtained doorway leading into the rest of the Kings' house. A screen door DSR opens onto the porch. An imaginary fourth wall separates the Kings' living room from the porch, which runs across the front of the house and faces the street. A glider and a chair are USC on the porch. At extreme DSR on the porch is a bench.

Steps lead from the porch up into Hattie's side of the house, which (in the interest of stage space and sight lines) is elevated above the Kings' side. A screen door opens into her foyer, which has a window on both the SR and the US sides. The former looks out onto a side street; the latter onto the back yard. The foyer opens into Hattie's living room, which is dominated by a piano USR and a piano bench. DSL is a rocking chair. SL is a small table with a telephone. USL is a console television with rabbit ears. A door USC leads off into the rest of her house.

In regard to decor, Hattie's living room is stiff and old-fashioned. The Kings' living room is furnished with an assortment of odds and ends, obviously put together catch-as-catch-can. Yet, it is tasteful in its own way and by no means garish.

# SYNOPSIS OF SCENES

## ACT I

### Scene 1
*A Saturday morning in May.*

### Scene 2
*A week or so later; 5:00 p.m.*

### Scene 3
*Two days later; 3:45 a.m.*

## ACT II

### Scene 1
*Two weeks later; late afternoon.*

### Scene 2
*Three days later; mid-to-late afternoon.*

### Scene 3
*Two days later; 3:00 a.m.*

### Scene 4
*A late afternoon in August, two months later.*

# THE ALTO PART

## ACT I
## Scene 1

*It is a Saturday morning in May. Lights come up on FLORENE KING'S side of the duplex. FLORENE, an attractive woman in her mid-to-late thirties, is dressing. She begins to sing in a blues voice reminiscent of Billie Holiday.*

FLORENE.
THERE'S A GARDEN WHERE THE FLOWERS
　ARE SENTIMENTAL HOURS,
THAT BLOOM ETERNALLY,
DOWN THE LANE OF LOVE,
IN THE GARDEN OF THE MOON
WHERE A COUPLE NEVER MISSES A CHANCE
　TO PICK SOME KISSES—1
*(As she starts to fasten her dress, she winces and grabs her back, interrupting her song.)* Oh! *(She tries to compose herself and finish her dressing and her song.)*
WHERE A COUPLE NEVER MISSES A CHANCE
　TO PICK SOME KISSES... 2
Now how does the rest of that go? *(She combs her mind for the words as she hums the melody, hoping to jog her memory. Meanwhile she is still trying to fasten her dress.)*

HUM-HUM-HUM-HUM-HUM-HUM...
Shoot! *(calling into next room)* Wanda! Will you come here a minute?

*(WANDA enters. She is a girl of twelve, but she still shows no visible signs of puberty. She is wearing a ruffled, organdy dress and nylon stockings that are far too big for her legs.)*

WANDA. Yes, ma'am?

FLORENE. Will you fasten this dress for me? That catch in my back grabs me every time I try to do it. *(WANDA fastens her mother's dress.)*

FLORENE. Wanda, you've heard me sing this song, haven't you? *(She sings.)*
THERE'S A GARDEN WHERE THE FLOWERS
 ARE SENTIMENTAL HOURS...3
"Garden of the Moon." I know I must have sung it to you.

WANDA. No, ma'am. I never heard it. But it sounds pretty.

FLORENE. It is. And now I can't remember all the words to it. That just kills me.

WANDA. *(She finishes fastening her mother's dress.)* Okay. You sure do look pretty.

FLORENE. Thank you, Honey. *(applying makeup)* I've got two new lines in my face.

WANDA. I don't see any. I wish I looked like you.

FLORENE. Aren't you sweet? *(examining her face again)* I hope King won't notice them. He ought to be here any minute now. Are you ready?

WANDA. Yes, ma'am. *(She waits for her mother to notice her* stockings, but *FLORENE is too preoccupied with her wrinkles.)* How do *I* look?

FLORENE. *(looking at her for the first time)* Cute — but what do you have on your legs?

WANDA. Your nylon stockings. You like them?

FLORENE. Those are women's stockings, Wanda, and too big for your little legs. You look like Olive Oyl.

WANDA. You mean I look silly?

FLORENE. Not silly — just little. You're still a child, Wanda. Don't rush things. I feel like I'm barely old enough to wear stockings myself. I'm sure not ready for you to.

WANDA. *(Deflated, she sits down on sofa and takes off the stockings.)* I look silly.

FLORENE. *(hugging her)* No, you don't. You look like my sweet little girl. And that's the way I want you to stay — for at least a while longer.

WANDA. *(Recovered, she gets up and starts dancing.)* I'm going to show him how I can bop.

FLORENE. Careful now. Remember these floors. And don't let Miz Hattie see you dancing.

WANDA. *(continuing to bop gingerly)* Why not?

FLORENE. She's a Baptist and doesn't believe in it. Well, I guess I'm ready. *(She scrutinizes her hair in the mirror over the dresser.)* I wonder why my hair never turns out like the hairdos in these magazines. *(She picks up a magazine from the coffee table and shows WANDA the hairdo she copied.)*

WANDA. I think it looks pretty.

FLORENE. You sure are good for my ego. *(She thumbs through the magazine.)* Oh, look at these pretty clothes! That's what I want — just as soon as King gets that championship belt.

WANDA. What I want is a t.v. of our own.
FLORENE. Oh, sure. We'll have to have one to watch your daddy before long. Yes, we'll get that right off the bat. And a big brick house of our own that nobody can sell out from under us. *(She rubs her back.)* I wish I hadn't tried to lift that heavy chifforobe by myself. I can't wait for him to get here and work this kink out of my back. *(WANDA starts to massage her mother's back.)* He's better than a chiropractor and doesn't charge either. I thought for certain he would have been here by now. I hope nothing's happened to him on the road. I've been dreaming about death left and right lately, and I'm as nervous as a cat. *(WANDA goes to the closet.)*
WANDA. I bet that Ouija board could tell us if he's all right. *(She pulls the Ouija board out of the closet.)* It knows everything. *(She crosses to the sofa with the board.)*
FLORENE. If that's so, then why would those people move out of here and leave it?
WANDA. I guess they found out all they needed to. *(She sits on sofa.)* Come on, Mama. *(FLORENE, at her direction, sits beside her.)* I know how to use it. All we do is place our fingers real light on this little thing. See? *(She puts her fingers on the planchette to show FLORENE, who does likewise.)*
FLORENE. Well, I suppose it wouldn't hurt. It'll keep us occupied till he gets here at least.
WANDA. I'll ask first, okay? *(She becomes very serious and concentrated.)* "Ouija, is Daddy all right?"
FLORENE. It's not doing anything.
WANDA. Wait, it will. There, it's moving.
FLORENE. Are you doing that, Wanda?

WANDA. No, ma'am. Are you?
FLORENE. I certainly am not. Where's it going?
WANDA. "Yes." It says Daddy is all right.
FLORENE. *(Breathing a sigh of relief.)* Whoooh! Good.
WANDA. Let me ask something else. "Ouija, will I be rich and famous?"
FLORENE. Look at that! It's going right to "Yes." Are you moving it, Wanda?
WANDA. No! See, I told you I'm going to be somebody.
FLORENE. Let me ask it something. "Ouija, will I ever get to sing?" It's moving. I take it back. I don't want to know. *(She shuts her eyes.)*
WANDA. It's too late.
FLORENE. I can't look.
WANDA. "Yes." It said "Yes," Mama.
FLORENE. *(She opens her eyes to see for herself.)* Well, my goodness, as old as I am. What do you know about that? You didn't move it, did you, Wanda?
WANDA. No, ma'am. Cross my heart. Now I'm going to ask one more thing. "Ouija, how old will I live to be and what will I die of?"
FLORENE. *(She jerks her fingers from the planchette.)* Wanda, don't you be asking about dying! You're just a kid. Besides, we're not supposed to know things like that.
WANDA. I don't see why not. I want to find out if it knows when people will die. Let me ask about somebody old.
FLORENE. Now, Wanda, don't nose into such ghoulish stuff.
WANDA. Let me test it on Miz Hattie. We'll write down

what it says, and then when she does die, we'll know whether to believe it about everything else.

FLORENE. Well, it would be nice to have a dependable source of advice. But Miz Hattie seems like a good enough landlady so far, and I don't want to think about her dying either. If she died, this house would probably sell, and we'd have to move again.

WANDA. Les ask it anyway. I bet it knows.

FLORENE. *(Tentatively placing her fingers on the planchette.)* I just couldn't face another move any time soon.

WANDA. "Ouija, we want to know about Miz Hattie now."

FLORENE. There's not another place in this town we could rent so cheap. And besides that, she lets us use her telephone and watch her t.v.

WANDA. Ssshhh! "Ouija, we want to know when Miz Hattie will die."

FLORENE. Wanda, this is spooky.

WANDA. Ssshhh! "S-O-O-N. Soon."

FLORENE. Oh, me. Well, we'll just have to leave that chifforobe here. "Ouija, are we going to have to move before next summer?" It's taking off. And my back is killing me.

WANDA. "No." It says "No," Mama.

FLORENE. How could that be — unless she left this place to us? Wanda. that must be it. Miz Hattie doesn't have any folks. I guess she's planning to make us her heirs. Well, this place could be fixed up. Les try to stay on the good side of her, Wanda, so she won't change her mind. *(WANDA has gotten up from the Ouija board and is writing in a tablet, which she takes from the coffee table.)* What are you doing?

ACT I　　　　　THE ALTO PART　　　　　15

WANDA. Writing down what the Ouija said so we can test it.

FLORENE. Our rent's due Monday, and I don't have the money for it. But what am I worrying about? King's going to have plenty in his pocket when he gets here. He's been having some good matches.

*(A car motor is heard.)*

FLORENE. Where is he? I'm just so anxious to see him.

WANDA. Mama, I heard a car. I bet that's him!

FLORENE. Thank goodness! Les get this put up quick.

*(She grabs the Ouija board and shoves it into closet as HATTIE'S telephone rings. Lights come up on HATTIE'S living room. HATTIE enters. She is seventy, a Republican, and a Baptist.)*

WANDA. *(looking out screen door)* Oh, phooey. It's just the postman.

HATTIE. *(picks up receiver)* Hello ... Who? ... I'll call her. *(She beats on her SL wall and shouts.)* Florene! Somebody's calling you long distance on my telephone

FLORENE. Oh, me!

HATTIE. *(shouting)* Florene!

FLORENE. *(shouting)* Yes, ma'am. I'm coming. *(To WANDA.)* I hope it's not the police calling to deliver a death message. *(FLORENE and WANDA exit from their living room and enter HATTIE'S side of the duplex.)*

HATTIE. Help yourself, Florene. I'm running late for my ride to Bible study.

FLORENE. Thank you, Miz Hattie. *(picks up receiver tentatively)* Hello? ... Oh, King! Thank goodness! Are you all right?

HATTIE. *(To WANDA, who is running her fingers lightly across the keys of the piano as she listens to the telephone conversation.)* Don't touch that. That belonged to Buddy Boy.

*(A car horn blows.)*

HATTIE. That's my ride, and I'm not ready. Wanda, run tell them I'm coming. *(WANDA reluctantly tears herself away from FLORENE'S conversation and starts toward the door.)* And see if the postman brought my Baptist Standard. I want to take it with me. *(WANDA exits. HATTIE hurriedly collects her purse and Bible.)*

FLORENE. Wichita Falls? ... Well, how wonderful!

HATTIE. Make sure you hang that up when you finish, Florene, and shut my front door. *(She exits to porch as WANDA runs up onto porch with mail in her hand. During the ensuing exchange between HATTIE and WANDA, FLORENE continues to talk on the telephone, but her conversation is not heard by the audience.)*

WANDA. They went on around the block to pick up Miz Davis. They'll be back. Here's your Baptist Standard. *(She starts back into HATTIE'S side of the house, but is detained by her.)*

HATTIE. I'd a been on time if ya'll hadn't got that phone call from Gorgeous George.

WANDA. He's not Gorgeous George. He's Killer King. Gorgeous George is sissified, and he's a *dirty* rassler. My daddy is a *clean* rassler.

HATTIE. What does that mean? That he don't stink? *(She cackles and swats WANDA'S shoulder with the Baptist Standard.)*

WANDA. *(wincing and rubbing her shoulder)* It means he follows the rules and doesn't cheat to win.

HATTIE. Then why's he got a name like Killer?

WANDA. It means Lady Killer. My daddy is real good looking.

HATTIE. Well, from what I see on the t.v., it all looks dirty to me. Grown men parading around half naked and a-showing their belly buttons.

WANDA. My daddy doesn't show his belly button.

HATTIE. *(not to be bested)* Don't you be messing with that piano now.

WANDA. Who was Buddy Boy anyhow?

HATTIE. My grandson.

WANDA. What happened to him?

HATTIE. Ole Roosevelt shipped him off to war and got him killed.

*(Car horn blows.)*

HATTIE. There's my ride. Make sure your mama pulls my door to good. *(exits)*

WANDA. *(bounding into HATTIE'S living room)* Mama, let me talk.

FLORENE. In a minute, Wanda. You know which song I'm talking about, King. I used to sing it all the time. *(sings)* "THERE'S A GARDEN WHERE THE FLOWERS ARE SENTIMENTAL HOURS..."4 ... You don't remember it? ... Oh, I was hoping you would.

WANDA. Mama!

FLORENE. Okay. Okay. Wanda wants to talk to you now ... I love you too. — Oh, and I'm real excited for you. *(passes receiver to WANDA)*

WANDA. Hi, Daddy! When are you coming? ... Ooooh. I had a lot of things to show you ... Oh, but I didn't get to ... Okay. Bye. Bye, Daddy. *(She hangs up.)* He ran out of change. I didn't even get to tell him I can bop. *(She cries.)*

FLORENE. Now, Wanda, don't act that way.

WANDA. He's not coming.

FLORENE. No, but listen, Wanda. They've routed him on a new circuit. All kinds of promoters are trying to book him. Your daddy's fixing to be famous, and we're going to have everything we want.

WANDA. *(still sniffling)* When?

FLORENE. Pretty soon now. Just pretty soon. Don't cry. He's going to be the champion. He's on his way to Wichita Falls. Then he'll go way out west to Abilene and Odessa and I don't know where all. Down to the border too. I bet he'll have a lot of good souvenirs when he does come. I'm just as excited as I can be. Now aren't you? ... Of course, I don't know what I'm going to do about our rent. He's had to put all his money into publicity, so he can't send any for a while.

WANDA. Uh-oh.

FLORENE. No, now. Everything's going to be all right. He told me to borrow the rent from Ola Belle. But I don't know if I can. Since she's started saving for that farm, I can't count on her anymore.

WANDA. What'll we do?

FLORENE. I'm going to apply King's philosophy: "Something will turn up." It works for him.

*(A car motor is heard.)*

FLORENE. Phew, les get out of here, Wanda. This place smells like Vicks Salve. It's making me sick at my stomach.
WANDA. Me, too.

*(They exit. The slam of a car door is heard. WANDA looks out from porch steps to see who it is.)*

WANDA. It's Aunt Ola Belle.
FLORENE. *(on porch now)* She's supposed to be at work. I wonder what she's doing here. Reckon fate sent her to loan me that rent money? *(She waves warmly to her sister, who is as yet unseen by the audience.)* Why, hello! What a surprise!

*(OLA BELLE enters wearing a white uniform. She is a large woman a few years older than FLORENE. Although her size would lead one to believe she could handle anything, she is now visibly shaken. Her hands are muddy, and there is a swipe of mud across her face.)*

OLA BELLE. Help me get inside!
FLORENE. What in the world is wrong? *(She and WANDA help OLA BELLE through their front door.)*
OLA BELLE. Let me set down! I'm shaking all over.
FLORENE. Are you sick?

OLA BELLE. Hell, no! Do you have any beer?

FLORENE. Beer? Why, no, I don't.

WANDA. Aunt Ola Belle, do you want me to get you a wet washrag to wash your face?

OLA BELLE. No, thank you, Sug. All that would really help me right now is a nice, cold beer. Well, anyway, I was on my way to work, and I ran into some light rain around Myrtle Springs. Then this big old rooster dashed out in front of me, and I threw on my brakes to keep from hitting him. The road was slicker than owlshit from the rain, and I didn't realize it. I want you to know that I skidded all over it and finally off of it and plowed into a mailbox.

FLORENE. Oh, no!

OLA BELLE. It's a good thing I hit it. If I hadn't, I might have gone right on into the ditch and turned over. I was completely out of control.

FLORENE. Did it mess up your car?

OLA BELLE. Hell, yes! I busted the headlight and tore off the fender. I'm on my way to the garage now to see how much damage was done.

WANDA. Mama, les go look at Aunt Ola Belle's car.

FLORENE. Not right now, Wanda. Won't your insurance pay for it?

OLA BELLE. Naw, all I've got is public liability. It just pays for the other feller you're in a wreck with. I doesn't provide for roosters and mailboxes.

FLORENE. Well, you have a lot saved, don't you?

OLA BELLE. Yes, but that's all for my farm. I'm scared to death Miz Ethyl will decide to sell it to somebody else before I can get enough together.

FLORENE. Oh, don't worry about that. Miz Ethyl doesn't need any money and never had even considered selling that place till you asked to buy it. You'd be perfectly safe to spend some of that money.

OLA BELLE. Hell, I don't want to. *(Crosses to mirror to assess the damages of the wreck on her.)* I can't wait to get out of that nut house.

FLORENE. Oh! ... Well, I don't see how you can stand to work with those crazy people anyhow. I certainly never could.

OLA BELLE. *(attempting to clean herself up)* I never thought I could either.

FLORENE. That just proves what I've always said — you're a lot stronger than I am. Yes, you'll be out of that asylum before you know it, and working your own farm. And maybe someday, some way I'll get to have a place of my own too.

WANDA. Mama, you will. Miz Hattie's going to die and leave us her house.

OLA BELLE. Well, isn't that grand?

FLORENE. Now, Wanda, we don't know that for sure.

WANDA. Yes, we do. The Ouija board told us, and I believe it. I'm going to be rich and famous, and Mama's going to get to sing.

FLORENE. I don't take it all that serious, Ola Belle, but it did put some ideas in my head. We know Miz Hattie's old, and according to the law of averages, she can't live a whole lot longer.

OLA BELLE. I wouldn't count on that. She looks to me like the kind they'll have to call up on Judgment Day and shoot.

FLORENE. If she *does* happen to die anytime soon, I think she might will this place to us. That may be why she's letting us rent it so cheap.

OLA BELLE. The reason she's letting you rent it cheap is that there's not a damned foundation under it, and any strong gust of wind could lift it off the building blocks. Florene, most people wouldn't live for free in a place where the floor shakes ever time you take a step.

FLORENE. It's not that bad if you walk light. It could be fixed up. And if we can just keep our rent paid on time, I think we have a good chance of getting it someday.

WANDA. Aunt Ola Belle, Daddy was supposed to come and bring us some money for the rent, but he had to go on to Wichita Falls.

OLA BELLE. I see. I wondered why ya'll were so dressed up. Wanda, I thought you wanted to see my car. I'm about to leave in a minute.

WANDA. Oh, okay. I'm going to go look. *(She exits.)*

OLA BELLE. So he'd still rather risk getting them pretty ears caulyflowered than take a reg'lar job so he can pay the rent.

FLORENE. He doesn't need a reg'lar job. He's a real good rassler.

OLA BELLE. Well, it seems to me like he's been twisting arms and busting butts an awful long time not to be any further along than he is.

FLORENE. He's just on the brink of success.

OLA BELLE. Then why didn't he send you some money?

FLORENE. He needed it for publicity. *(During the following exchange with OLA BELLE, FLORENE changes out of her nice clothes into an everyday dress.)*

OLA BELLE. And I need my damned money to get my car fixed and buy my farm.

FLORENE. I didn't ask you for any money.

OLA BELLE. No, you just stood around like a dying calf in a hailstorm waiting for me to rescue you.

FLORENE. I don't need your help. You just want to believe that so you'll feel important.

OLA BELLE. Bullshit!

FLORENE. My husband will provide for me.

OLA BELLE. Just like he provided for Papa.

FLORENE. Leave Papa out of this.

OLA BELLE. Oh how I wish he had been left out of it! If King hadn't talked Papa into mortgaging his cafe to finance that second-rate rassling career, I'd be raising beautiful things on my farm right now with the money I got from my part of it when Papa died — instead of having a corral a bunch of idiots for a living. And you could be in a house that didn't shake like a by-God leaf in the wind.

FLORENE. I'm not complaining.

OLA BELLE. I guess you're happy then with the way things are.

FLORENE. Yes! Yes, I am! I'm as happy as a lark! And don't you try to make me think I'm not! You're the one that's unhappy and soured out on life.

OLA BELLE. I got cheated, and I'm mad about it.

FLORENE. It's not my fault you didn't get a husband.

OLA BELLE. And by God and Jesus, it ain't my fault you did. You picked him, Florene, and you can take the consequences. I've thrown out the lifeline to you for the last time.

*(Picks up her purse to go just as WANDA re-enters.)*

WANDA. Boy, Aunt Ola Belle, your car sure is a mess. I never knew a rooster could cause so much damage.

OLA BELLE. Sug, there just ain't no end to the trouble they can cause.

*(She exits through screen door just as ETHYL enters porch area from outside. ETHYL is an unmarried woman in her sixties. Although she is a spinster, her heart has not hardened. She is carrying a large painting. FLORENE and WANDA exit through their USL doorway.)*

ETHYL. Oh, Ola Belle! How are you, Honey? I came to show my oil painting to Florene, but I'll let you see it too. *(Extends painting to OLA BELLE, who examines it.)*

OLA BELLE. You did this?

ETHYL. I sure did.

OLA BELLE. What's it supposed to be?

ETHYL. I'm calling it "Racccoon under a Tree."

OLA BELLE. *(studying the painting)* Oh, *I* see. That's a *big* coon, Miz Ethyl. Real good though.

ETHYL. Thank you, Honey. But I'm getting tired of wildlife. I'm going to see if I can get Florene to pose for my next painting.

OLA BELLE. That should be right up her alley. She loves to be the center of attention. Don't sell that farm now till I get enough saved to buy it. *(exits)*

ETHYL. *(calling after her)* Okay, Honey. *(examines the painting again)* These colors really perk up in the sunshine. *(calling inside to FLORENE)* Florene? Florene, can you come out here? I want to show you something in the light.

*(FLORENE enters porch area, checking to make sure OLA BELLE has gone.)*

FLORENE. Hello, Miz Ethyl.
ETHYL. Hello, Honey. Oh, don't you look pretty? Lissen, I want you to pose for me so I can paint you in oils.

*(WANDA joins them on the porch.)*

WANDA. Hi, Miz Ethyl.
ETHYL. Hello, Little Miss. I'm going to paint your mama's picture.
WANDA. Oh boy! Can I watch?
ETHYL. I'm not fixing to do it right now. But you can when I start. I have to decide first how I want to show her.
WANDA. Show her singing.
ETHYL. Ooohh. I don't think I know how to do that. I can't paint a mouth closed — much less open. I'd like to show that she's the wife of a rassler, but I don't know how to do that either. Here's what I want to show you now, though. My wildlife painting! *(She shows them.)*
FLORENE. Oh, that's pretty, Miz Ethyl. You did a good job on this cow, didn't she Wanda?

WANDA. Yes, ma'am.

ETHYL. That's not a cow. That's a coon. Maybe I got it too big. But I couldn't get him to pose — wouldn't sit still at all. I just had to do this from memory and imagination. That's why it will be nice to have you pose for me, Florene.

*(A passing truck is heard as all heads turn to look.)*

WANDA. Look at that moving van. Somebody new must be coming to town.

FLORENE. Looks like whoever it is has a lot of furniture. That's a long van. I bet they can afford to hire somebody to do their lifting.

ETHYL. Reckon who it is? *(They all watch the van go out of sight.)* Florene, just as soon as I can figger out how I want to show you, I'll be ready to get started.

FLORENE. Okay, Miz Ethyl. I guess I'm not going anywhere.

ETHYL. *(starts to leave)* Bye-bye. I'm going to go call Velma Bateman. If there's a vacant house where that moving van might be going, she'll know it. *(exits)*

FLORENE. Goodbye, Miz Ethyl. *(sits in glider)* It will be nice to have my picture painted ... But that was way out of proportion, wasn't it, Wanda? *(WANDA nods as she too sits in the glider.)* I hope she won't paint me that big. I don't want to be remembered as a fat lady. *(They sit together in silence for a few moments.)*

WANDA. I didn't even get to talk to him. I've changed a bunch since he was here at Christmas ... I wish he lived at home.

FLORENE. And worked in a filling station or a dry goods store? Wanda, you don't want a daddy like that. Don't even think it. He's going to make all our dreams come true. *(WANDA does not look entirely convinced. FLORENE attempts to divert her.)* Look, Wanda! *(points across the street)* The Hendersons are back from their honeymoon.

WANDA. *(drawing in her breath)* Aaah! He kissed her! Where did they go anyhow?

FLORENE. *(longingly)* Galveston, Miz Ethyl said.

WANDA. Wow, Galveston! Where you and Daddy had your picture made.

FLORENE. Uh-huh.

WANDA. And you got to wade in the Gulf of Mexico.

FLORENE. Why, yes, I did, Wanda! I had forgotten about that!

WANDA. And Daddy won his best match and everybody said he'd be the champion. And then he took you to the night club.

FLORENE. And bought me a orchid corsage to pin in my hair.

WANDA. And you wore a black sequin dress.

FLORENE. Yes. King had just bought that for me in Houston. And he wore his white linen suit. Oh, he was good looking!

WANDA. What's it like in a night club?

FLORENE. Elegant ... Real elegant. Lots of colored lights. Pretty music. Fancy cocktails. I had something called a sloe gin fizz. I ordered it because I liked the way it sounded, but it tasted good too. And made me feel warm and relaxed all over. I wish I had one now. Then King had the band play a song I knew, and he made me get up and sing — on a stage with a spotlight and microphone and everything.

WANDA. Weren't you scared?

FLORENE. Not one bit. Everything was so easy that night, Wanda. I didn't even have to try. It seemed like the words just poured out of my mouth. Even the band leader told me how good I was.

WANDA. I wasn't even born yet. All the good stuff happened before I was there to enjoy it.

FLORENE. Poor Wanda. I wish you *had* been there so you could reminisce with me. And jog my memory about the things I'm forgetting.

WANDA. I don't forget anything. I have a photographic memory — practically.

FLORENE. I used to too, before I had so much on my mind. Why don't you memorize all my old songs, Wanda? I could teach them to you. We could sing together, too. *(WANDA shakes her head.)* Why don't you try?

WANDA. I couldn't be as good as you.

FLORENE. You don't have to make a career out of it. This would be strictly for fun — just the two of us.

WANDA. What song did you sing at that nightclub?

FLORENE. Oh, that was King's favorite — "Maybe." You've heard me sing it a million times. I bet you already know it.

WANDA. Yes, ma'am. I think so.

FLORENE. Okay, then. We'll start with that one. *(She sings a few words to get WANDA started, but lets WANDA sing alone when she seems confident of the words and melody.)*

FLORENE and WANDA.

MAYBE YOU'LL THINK OF ME,

WHEN YOU ARE ALL ALONE,5
> FLORENE. See, you have a sweet voice.
> WANDA. Really?
> FLORENE. Yes. Les do some more.
> FLORENE and WANDA.

MAYBE THE ONE WHO IS WAITING FOR YOU
  WILL PROVE UNTRUE
THEN WHAT WILL YOU DO.6
> WANDA. *(stops singing)* I can't do it with you. You sing too good and drown me out.
>
> FLORENE. Oh, for goodness sake. Well, we'll do harmony then and sing different parts. You sing the melody just like you were doing, and I'll take the alto part. That way I won't overpower you. Okay?
>
> WANDA. I guess so.
>
> FLORENE. Start it from the beginning. *(WANDA starts singing the melody, and FLORENE joins her singing the alto part.)*
>
> FLORENE and WANDA.

MAYBE YOU'LL THINK OF ME,
WHEN YOU ARE ALL ALONE,7
*(WANDA drops into FLORENE'S alto part with her.)*
> FLORENE. Now stay with the melody, Wanda. It's a temptation to sing what the other person's singing, but you have to stick to your part to make the song work. Okay, les go on. We're sounding real good.
>
> FLORENE and WANDA. *(in harmony)*

MAYBE THE ONE WHO IS WAITING FOR YOU
  WILL PROVE UNTRUE
THEN WHAT WILL YOU DO....8
*(As lights go down.)*

# Scene 2

*A week or so later. 5:00 p.m. Lights up on Kings' living room. Sounds of children leaving school drift in. FLORENE is alone and standing at an ironing board ironing. Freshly ironed dresses, blouses, and skirts hang all about the room. The dress she is finishing up is a ruffled one, starched stiff, and obviously hard to iron. She struggles with it and wipes perspiration. The radio is on, playing a popular song of the time, ideally something swelling and romantic. FLORENE finishes the dress and starts to hang it up, but stops to hold it in front of her and to look at herself in the mirror. Just as the song crescendos to its end, ETHYL bounds up onto porch.*

ETHYL. *(calling)* Wanda? *(Goes to FLORENE'S screen door.)*
FLORENE. Come in, Miz Ethyl. *(ETHYL enters. FLORENE turns off radio.)* She's not home from school yet. I hope nothing's happened to her.
ETHYL. I came to tell her that she's getting a new music teacher. You know that long moving van we saw the other day? Well, it was carrying her stuff. She's Velma Bateman's neighbor.
FLORENE. What happened to the music teacher they had?
ETHYL. Oh, she had a nervous breakdown. Life's full of sad surprises, isn't it?

FLORENE. It sure is. Did you know Miz Hattie's turned as mean as a snake?

ETHYL. No!

FLORENE. Yes, ma'am. She insulted our singing and dunned me for the rent.

ETHYL. Why, the very idea! Ya'll sound good enough to be on Toast of the Town.

FLORENE. Thank you. Miz Hattie said she wished we *were* on the t.v. so she could turn us off.

ETHYL. I am just flabbergasted. She used to love singing. Her and Buddy Boy spent many a hour singing hymns and playing the piano. Oh ... I bet that's it.

FLORENE. What?

ETHYL. Ya'll may have stirred up some memories. She doesn't like to think about him. He was going to be a preacher. She had big plans for his life — just like you all do, Florene. I hope you'll remember me after Mr. King's a well-known rassler, and you go to singing in public. *(Indicating the clothes FLORENE is ironing.)* You sure do have some beautiful clothes, Florene.

FLORENE. Oh, these are not—

ETHYL. Yes, there's just something special about everything you do.

FLORENE. Why, thank you, Miz Ethyl.

ETHYL. Well, I'm not going to be able to wait for Wanda. I have to go get set up to paint while there's still some light. I'm working on a apple that's about to rot on me. Bye now, Honey. *(She exits.)*

FLORENE. Bye, Miz Ethyl.

*(She looks at clock on fourth wall and then out the door. Then she*

*starts to put away the ironing board. At that moment Wanda races up onto porch calling to her mother.)*

WANDA. Mama! *(enters with her schoolbooks and lunch box)* Mama, guess what?
FLORENE. Where have you been? I was worried to death.
WANDA. I have perfect pitch! She kept me after school to work with me in the music hall. She said I am the best singer in the whole school!
FLORENE. *(still putting away the ironing board)* Who said that, Wanda?
WANDA. She did — our new music teacher. Boy, it's hot in here. I wish we had an air conditioner. She tested us, and I got the highest score. Think of that, Mama! Perfect pitch!
FLORENE. That's nice. Means you can sing on key. I never was tested, but I expect mine is perfect too.
WANDA. She worked with me quite a bit and had me sing scales up and down the piano. I sang her one of your old songs too.
FLORENE. Wanda! Those are just supposed to be for us.
WANDA. She loved it. She thinks I ought to go to college and major in music. Wouldn't that be something? *(She takes off her shoes.)*
FLORENE. It sure would. That would cost an awful lot of money ... Which song did you sing?
WANDA. "Deep Purple." I'm thinking about U.C.L.A.
FLORENE. What gave you that idea? Do you even know where it is?

WANDA. Sure. I read about it in *Photoplay*. Some of the stars went there. It's close to Hollywood.

FLORENE. Now, Wanda, you know you can't afford to go to a movie-star school.

WANDA. Mama, by the time I get ready to go, Daddy will have the championship rasslin' belt. Then I can do anything I want to.

FLORENE. I sure hope he will, Wanda, but don't get too carried away now. Here you have known this woman one day, and you're already making plans to leave me and go away off to California. I never saw you like this before.

WANDA. Well, I never knew anybody like her. I guess she's the prettiest woman I ever saw. She dresses up to come to school just like it was Easter Sunday at church. Today she had on this apricot-colored taffeta sleeveless dress with a three-quarter-length sleeve bolero.

FLORENE. It must be nice to be able to dress like that. Does she have a rich husband?

WANDA. No. She makes plenty of money to do anything she wants to. And she can have a date anytime she wants one.

FLORENE. She certainly toots her own horn, doesn't she? How old is this lady, Wanda?

WANDA. I heard she's twenty-nine, but she looks a whole lot younger than that. She doesn't look a bit old.

FLORENE. I guess not. I didn't either when I was that age.

WANDA. Were you thinking about singing then?

FLORENE. Yes. I always have been.

WANDA. But you never did anything about it.

FLORENE. *(hurt and defensive)* I never had a chance!

WANDA. Mama, she thinks I ought to take singing lessons. Can I?

FLORENE. What? Lessons? No, Wanda. I don't think so ... How much would that cost?

WANDA. Just $3.00 a lesson.

FLORENE. That's a lot of money. We just couldn't afford that right now.

WANDA. Mama, I don't see why not. I bet Daddy will let me.

FLORENE. Now, Wanda, you can't jump into something like that.

WANDA. Why not?

FLORENE. You just can't. We can't even pay the rent.

WANDA. But, Mama, she say's I'm talented!

FLORENE. I can't help it. Your daddy's trying to get established in his career. Once he gets where he needs to be, then everything will be different.

WANDA. It might be too late then. He'll find a way if I ask him.

FLORENE. No, he won't!

WANDA. Yes, he will!

FLORENE. He'll say yes, and then leave it up to me to find a way! *(catches herself)* Of course he'd find a way if he could. But he can't. That's all.

*(The sound of a car stopping outside is heard.)*

WANDA. *(defiantly)* I'm going to write my daddy. *(Gets pencil and paper from coffee table and flings herself dramatically on sofa, starting to write.)*

*(A car door slams.)*

FLORENE. *(looking out door)* Now I want you to straighten up, Wanda. Somebody's coming to the door. And she drives a convertible.

*(ALTHEA LOCKWOOD enters porch area. She is a pretty, dramatic woman in her late twenties. She wears the apricot taffeta dress described earlier by WANDA. FLORENE hurriedly tries to tidy up things. WANDA keeps on writing. ALTHEA knocks at their door. FLORENE calls.)*

FLORENE. Just a minute! Wanda, put your shoes on.
WANDA. What for? What's so hot about this old lady?
FLORENE. *(swatting at her legs as she goes to the door)* You mind me, Wanda! *(opens door)* Hello, Miz Lockwood. Come on in. I just finished your ironing. *(WANDA'S jaw drops as she hears the name of her music teacher and looks up to see her. She would flee, but realizes it is too late. She is scrambling to put on her shoes and straighten her hair and clothes as ALTHEA LOCKWOOD sweeps in.)*
ALTHEA. Mrs. King, I am so happy to find somebody to do my ironing. I had a Nigra woman who used to do it for me in Greenville, and I was afraid I couldn't get anybody to do it here. *(sees WANDA)* Why, Wanda! What a surprise! Don't tell me this is your mother?
WANDA. *(wishing it were not so)* Yes, ma'am.
ALTHEA. I should have connnected you all by your last

names, but it just never entered my mind.

FLORENE. I guess you must be Wanda's new music teacher. You didn't mention that when you came by yesterday. She's already described your dress in such detail that I couldn't fail to recognize it.

ALTHEA. Oh, don't you love this ensemble? I had it made to order for me. There are six yards in the skirt alone.

FLORENE. I don't doubt it. All your skirts are full. — Would you like to sit down and have a glass of ice tea, Miz Lockwood?

ALTHEA. How sweet of you to offer, Mrs. King! But I have to run. I'm driving to Greenville tonight to see my fiancé's band perform.

WANDA. Is he a orchestra leader?

ALTHEA. No, Dear. He's a band director at the school where I used to teach before I went back for my Master's of Art degree. He has the best band in the state, bar none. They've never gotten less than a "1" in anything.

FLORENE. *(determined not to be impressed)* I'll say.

WANDA. I'm going to be in the band as soon as I can get a horn.

ALTHEA. Good! But I don't want that to interfere with your singing. Did Wanda tell you, Mrs. King, that she is musically gifted and ought to be developing her voice?

FLORENE. Yes, she did, Miz Lockwood. That's real nice, but we won't be able to afford lessons for her right now.

WANDA. Mama! I told you I'm writing my daddy, and he'll let me. *(to ALTHEA)* My daddy will let me take those lessons, Miz Lockwood.

ALTHEA. I should hope so. It would be a shame for talent like yours to go to waste. The only unpardonable mistake in life, as far as I am concerned, is not living up to out potential. Besides, it's rare to find a gifted young voice to develop.

WANDA. See, Mama.

FLORENE. Like I said before, we just can't afford the lessons.

ALTHEA. Why don't you let Wanda ask her daddy the way she wants to, Mrs. King? Isn't it a daddy's pleasure to humor his little girl?

WANDA. See, Mama. *(FLORENE glares at WANDA.)*

ALTHEA. What line of work is your husband in, Mrs. King?

FLORENE. He's a rassler.

ALTHEA. A wrestler? Uh, well — how unusual!

WANDA. He calls himself Killer King, and he's going to win the championship belt. *(Takes a picture from dresser to show ALTHEA.)* See, here's a picture of him in his trunks.

ALTHEA. My goodness! He's a large man, isn't he? And muscular! *(Reluctant to hand back the picture, but ashamed of her interest.)*

FLORENE. *(Taking the picture from her and returning it to dresser.)* Yes, there's nothing sissified about my husband.

ALTHEA. Well, you ask him, Wanda, about those lessons. Tell him *how important* it is for you to take them.

WANDA. Yes, ma'am, I will. *(FLORENE starts gathering*

*up the ironed clothes.)*

ALTHEA. How much do I owe you, Mrs. King?

FLORENE. I don't ususally do this sort of thing, so I don't know. But I guess I should charge by the piece. *(calculates)* That'll be $2.50. Does that seem fair to you?

ALTHEA. That's a little more than my Nigra woman used to charge — but I bet you do a better job on ruffles than she did. Here you are, Mrs. King. *(takes money from change purse and hands it to her)* I'll bring you my clothes again next Thursday? *(takes ironed clothes from FLORENE)*

FLORENE. *(grimly)* That'll be fine.

ALTHEA. Bye now, Wanda. *(As she starts to exit, she calls back over her shoulder.)* Write that letter! *(exits)*

WANDA. How could you embarrass me like that? Taking in ironing! And from my music teacher!

FLORENE. I didn't know who she was. She had an ad in the paper, and I called her.

*(Sound of departing car is heard.)*

WANDA. This is the best thing that's ever happened to me, and now it's ruined.

FLORENE. Lissen, Wanda, you selfish thing, I was ironing for your benefit too. And believe me, it was no fun!

WANDA. I just hope she'll still want to teach me.

FLORENE. Don't worry. She will. But you still won't have the money for lessons.

WANDA. Yes, I will. I'm going to finish this letter like Miz Lockwood told me to.

FLORENE. Go ahead! Just go ahead! But don't you *ever* sing "Deep Purple" with her again! You hear me! Or any other song I taught you! *(WANDA scribbles out the rest of her letter as FLORENE sits down and props up her feet. The air between them is charged. They do not speak for a long time. Finally FLORENE can bear the silence no longer.)* I've got two more ironings lined up for tomorrow. I hope they won't be people you're trying to impress. At least I can give Miz Hattie part of the rent money if King doesn't send us some.

WANDA. *(finishes letter and seals envelope)* There! *(A few more moments of silence.)*

FLORENE. I wonder what Miz Hattie's not going to let us see on her t.v. tonight.

WANDA. *(looking at newspaper)* It's a mystery theatre. Oooh, look what's on at the picture show! It's that new movie we saw the previews of starring Jennifer Jones.

FLORENE. What's that?

WANDA. *Love Is a Many Splendored Thing.*

FLORENE. Oh, yes. Sounds good, doesn't it?

WANDA. Ooooh, I'll die if I don't get to see it. It's supposed to be better than *Gone with the Wind.*

FLORENE. Who else is in it?

WANDA. That actor that you think looks like Daddy.

FLORENE. William Holden?

WANDA. Yes, ma'am. Oh, Mama—

FLORENE. Well, it would only be forty-five cents. I guess that much wouldn't keep Miz Hattie from throwing us out.

WANDA. So, can we? Can we?

FLORENE. We might as well. And les don't be mad at each other any more. If we leave right now, we can see the early show. That way we won't have to be walking home so late. *(She starts to dash off a note.)* We'll just have to eat supper when we get back. I'm leaving this note in case anybody is looking for us. *(She fastens the note to the screen-door with a bobby pin.)* Come on. We don't want to miss the previews.

*(They exit. The lights have gradually faded to twilight by the time they decide to see the movie and leave. A car is heard stopping, and the car door slams. OLA BELLE bounds up onto the porch wearing her white uniform and carrying a six-pack of beer. The set is now in night light.)*

OLA BELLE. *(calling into Kings' side of house)* Florene? Wanda? Is anybody at home? Come on out and les bury the hatchet. *(Notices note and removes it from screen door so she can read it.)* "Have gone to see *Love Is a Many Splendored Thing.* Florene and Wanda." Well, shit. The one time I have good news, there's not anybody to tell it to. *(Goes up steps and peers into HATTIE'S door.)* Wonder if that old sister's here? Dudn't look like it. *(Comes back down steps and sits in glider. She opens a can of beer and drinks it as she swings.)*

ETHYL. *(Calling from offstage.)* Hattie, is that you?

*(ETHYL enters.)*

OLA BELLE. Naw, it's the booger man.
ETHYL. Ola Belle, what are you doing a'setting out here by yourself?
OLA BELLE. Drinking beer and having the time of my life. Come get in on the fun. *(She moves over in glider so*

*ETHYL can sit beside her.)*

ETHYL. *(sitting)* I guess Hattie must be at the revival. Wonder where Florene and Wanda's at?

OLA BELLE. Oh, they're at the picture show seeing a love story. What brings you out so late?

ETHYL. I just heard the *best* piece of news of my party line and couldn't wait till morning to tell it!

OLA BELLE. Well, les hear it. And then I've got something to tell you. But we better have a beer first. *(Opens a beer and hands it to ETHYL.)*

ETHYL. Oh, no, I never—

OLA BELLE. Come on. We're celebrating good news, ain't we?

ETHYL. Well, I guess it wouldn't hurt to *try* one. I've been wondering how it tastes ever since I read in *True Story* about a girl going to a beer party. *(takes a beer)* Of course, she got into all kinds of trouble afterwards. *(She sips it cautiously.)*

OLA BELLE. How you like it?

ETHYL. It's a whole lot like soapsuds, isn't it? But it's cold. Well, here's what I heard: Sparta's fixing to get a art teacher. Isn't that exciting? A retired commercial artist from Dallas they said. Teaches oils and pastels both. And it wouldn't surprise me a bit if he was a Frenchman to boot.

OLA BELLE. So you're going to take one of his classes?

ETHYL. Oh, no! I'm afraid to. I'm not good enough.

OLA BELLE. Then what are you so excited about?

ETHYL. Just knowing that if I get good enough, maybe he'll teach me someday. Show me how to paint things the way they are.

OLA BELLE. Sounds like a lot of ifs and maybes to me, but if it makes you happy, I'll drink to that. *(Clinks her beer against ETHYL'S.)*

ETHYL. Thank you, Honey. Now I want to hear what you're celebrating.

OLA BELLE. I got a raise today — that I didn't even expect.

ETHYL. Good for you! *(Clinks her beer against OLA BELLE'S.)* It couldn't happen to a nicer girl. I always knew you'd be a success. I bet they make you a warden before long and give you a gun and everything.

OLA BELLE. They're not wardens, Miz Ethyl. They're supervisors. And I'm not going to be one.

ETHYL. Honey, if you take that attitude, you won't be. But I believe you can go as high in that asylum as you want to.

OLA BELLE. Miz Ethyl, listen. I don't want to go high there. What I'm celebrating is that I'll be able to quit even sooner than I thought and buy that farm from you.

ETHYL. Oh! Well, I know you must be happy.

OLA BELLE. I keep thinking I will be. But ever since they told me about that raise today, I've been worried about what they was planning to make me do to pay for it.

ETHYL. Oooh! *(Her imagination going wild.)* What do you suppose they have in mind?

OLA BELLE. A transfer to a different ward. How about another beer, Miz Ethyl? *(Opens a new beer for each of them.)* See, I've been on Ward K now for two years.

ETHYL. *(wide-eyed)* What's on Ward K?

OLA BELLE. All the pissers. Not to mention the screamers and the wall climbers.

ETHYL. Mercy! Where do you think they'll send you now?

OLA BELLE. I figger Ward X.

ETHYL. Lordy! How did you get into that line of work?

OLA BELLE. Seems like I was snatched out of the cradle and put in this uniform. But actually I started there after Papa lost the cafe and died, and I'd had my fling at California.

ETHYL. At least you've had a fling. And you work on those wards where anything can happen. Here I am old enough to die, and I've never done a thing exciting.

OLA BELLE. Well, hell, you'd better get after it then, Miz Ethyl. Time's a wasting. You better do something wild.

ETHYL. I don't know what to do. Never have.

OLA BELLE. Don't think about it. Just cut loose. Like you are now with this beer. Damn! You're a good sport. You'd sure never catch Old Lady Hattie doing anything like that.

ETHYL. My goodness, I forgot all about her.

OLA BELLE. Good. That's the way you start being wild.

ETHYL. But if she walked up and saw us drinking beer on her front porch, she'd have a heart attack. Oh, me!

OLA BELLE. Quit worrying about her — or anybody else.

ETHYL. She *might* die. *(She is drunk enough now to find this very funny. So does OLA BELLE.)* She has heart trouble. But

I'm not supposed to tell it. And here I have. You won't repeat it, will you?

OLA BELLE. Hell, no. I'm probably too drunk to remember it.

ETHYL. I wonder if I'm drunk.

OLA BELLE. Probably. But don't give it a thought. If you're going to be wild, you just have to jump in with both feet.

ETHYL. Oh, Honey, do you reckon I could?

OLA BELLE. Hell, yes! I'm telling you so. You're done on the road.

ETHYL. Ola Belle, you've inspired me. *(rises from glider)* I wish I could stay on a while, but I have to hurry home to the bathroom. I guess it's all this exciting talk. *(Exits hastily, but calls back over her shoulder.)* Don't you worry now about that Old Ward X!

OLA BELLE. *(alone)* I'm not. I've already had too much beer to care.

*(Lights go down.)*

## Scene 3

*Two days later. 3:45 a.m. Lights up on Kings' living room. WANDA is asleep on sofa. FLORENE enters briskly through USL doorway from the back of the house. She is dressed up and carrying clothes and toilet items, which she*

ACT I   THE ALTO PART   45

> *begins to pack into a small suitcase. She sings — not loud enough to be heard by HATTIE, but with the intention of waking WANDA.)*

FLORENE.
SAY, IT'S ONLY A PAPER MOON,
SAILING OVER A CARDBOARD SEA,9
   WANDA. *(Rouses a little and moans.)* Ssssh!
   FLORENE.
BUT IT WOULDN'T BE MAKE BELIEVE,
IF YOU BELIEVED IN ME.10
*(Goes to table by sofa and turns on lamp and then returns to her packing.)*
YES, IT'S ONLY A CANVAS SKY,
HANGING OVER A MUSLIN TREE,11
   WANDA. *(opening one eye)* What time is it?
   FLORENE.
BUT IT WOULDN'T BE MAKE BELIEVE,
IF YOU BELIEVED IN ME.12
   WANDA. It seems like the middle of the night. The stars are still out.
   FLORENE.
...IT'S ONLY A PAPER MOON,
SAILING OVER A CARDBOARD SEA....13
   WANDA. *(squints at clock)* It's not even 4:00 clock. I'm going back to sleep.
   FLORENE. You better get up. Your breakfast is getting cold.
   WANDA. I don't want any.
   FLORENE. You'll get carsick if you don't eat something.

WANDA. *I'm* not going anywhere!

FLORENE. Aren't you going with Ola Belle when she takes me to catch the bus?

WANDA. No! *(covers her head)*

FLORENE. Suit yourself. I hope I'm taking enough clothes. I wonder if I'll need a evening dress.

WANDA. *(uncovers her head)* You're not going to a night club!

FLORENE. How do you know? There's no telling what we'll do.

WANDA. *(sits up)* Why can't I come, Mama?

FLORENE. You'd have to miss school. Besides, we can't afford two tickets ... I'm going to have King buy me a cocktail tonight. I think I'll try a martini.

WANDA. He doesn't even know you're coming. What if you get lost?

FLORENE. I've got the address of his rooming house. I can always ask a policeman. *(sings)*
BUT IT WOULDN'T BE MAKE BELIEVE,
IF YOU BELIEVED IN ME.14

WANDA. *(gets out of bed)* I haven't missed but one day of school all year. My teachers wouldn't care if I took off to go to Wichita Falls.

FLORENE. You don't have a ticket.

WANDA. Aunt Ola Belle will buy me one if I ask her. It can be for my Christmas present. *(with animation)* I'm coming with you! There's no reason why I can't! *(She begins to grab clothes from her closet.)* I'll wear pedal pushers on the bus.

FLORENE. Put those things back, Wanda. You're not going anywhere.

WANDA. Yes, I am. *(FLORENE takes the clothes from her and puts them back in the closet. While FLORENE is not looking, WANDA takes an envelope from coffee table and slips it into FLORENE'S suitcase.)* Why can't I?

FLORENE. Because you have to stay here and kowtow to that music teacher.

WANDA. I do not!

FLORENE. Yes, you do. I want you and her to do plenty of talking about that picture show and learn to sing the sheet music together while I'm gone.

WANDA. I can't sing it. It's too high for my voice.

FLORENE. But I bet it's not for hers. She can probably sing high enough to split your eardrums.

WANDA. She sings good. She's trained her voice. She spent a summer abroad studying opera.

FLORENE. She looks like the type that would want to sing opera.

WANDA. She likes all kinds of singing. Musicals, too. She's even seen some shows on Broadway.

FLORENE. I tell you, I don't know how Sparta managed till she got here.

WANDA. I don't see why you're mad at her.

FLORENE. I'm not mad at her! I'm mad at you! You deceived me, Wanda. Talked me into spending my hard-earned ironing money to take you to the picture show. And let me think you wanted us to see it together so we could have it to remember for a long time to come, like we always have when we saw picture shows.

WANDA. I wanted us to see it.

FLORENE. Hah! I might as well have stayed at home. Once we got there all you did was talk about Althea Lockwood and *her* interpretation of it. You never once asked me my opinion.

WANDA. She knows all about it. She saw it in Dallas and got the sheet music.

FLORENE. But I'm the one that knows about love and romance, Wanda! Can't you understand that? I'm the one that's married to a man that looks like William Holden, and that's on his way to making our dreams come true. Me! Not her! And you're acting like she's an authority on it!

WANDA. She is. She read the book.

FLORENE. How could she know anything about love? She's spent all her time getting degrees and sashaying around the world.

WANDA. She's engaged.

FLORENE. Then why wasn't she wearing an engagement ring? Answer me that. No, Wanda, Miz Lockwood *has* to settle for picture shows and sheet music and books about love.

WANDA. She does not! Her life is perfect! And I'm going to be just like her.

FLORENE. I think you already are. She can't have the real thing. And neither can you.

*(Car is heard stopping outside, followed by door slam.)*

FLORENE. But I can. And I'm on my way to Wichita Falls.

WANDA. *(hurt beneath her fury)* I'm going to go eat my breakfast.

*(She exits. FLORENE continues to pack, but her bravado attitude fades once WANDA leaves the room. OLA BELLE enters onto porch and starts to knock, but FLORENE intercepts her and opens door.)*

FLORENE. *(talking low)* Good morning. *(OLA BELLE enters wearing a rumpled white uniform and houseshoes and carrying an overnight bag.)* Try not to wake up the old hussy. She doesn't know I'm going. Did you get any sleep?

OLA BELLE. I took a nap after I got in at 12:00. But I didn't bother to get undressed.

FLORENE. It sure is nice of you to see me off so early. And to stay here with Wanda while I'm gone.

OLA BELLE. I can afford to be nice. Things are working out in my favor lately. Besides, I didn't want to miss this momentous occasion. This is the first time you *ever* went off by yourself, Florene.

FLORENE. I'm just mad enough to do anything. Wanda tricked me into taking her to see *Love Is a Many Splendored Thing*.

OLA BELLE. Well, hell, I knew by the title alone that wasn't going to be nothing but a tub of horseshit.

FLORENE. Oh, no. It was wonderful. So sad. It's just that — well, Wanda's turned against me. That's all. And I need to see King.

OLA BELLE. I hope you're not using that rent money I loaned you to finance this trip.

FLORENE. I'm not. *(proudly)* I'm paying for it with my own money.

OLA BELLE. Where'd you get any money?

FLORENE. I made it. Ironing for people.

OLA BELLE. God-a-Mighty! *(shakes her head)* I hope it's worth it. *(She reflects a few moments and then reaches into her purse and takes out two dollars, which she hands to FLORENE.)* Here, kid, this is for your eats on the trip.

FLORENE. Ola Belle, I can't let you do that. I've already fixed myself a lunch to have on the bus. *(Indicates paper sack on table by sofa.)*

OLA BELLE. You take it. It might come in handy. If you don't need it for anything else, you can bring Wanda back a souvenir.

FLORENE. Well, okay. Thank you.

OLA BELLE. It's my job to take care of crazy people — whether they're in the asylum or not.

*(WANDA enters, eating a piece of toast. She has put on a duster over her nightgown. She is still furious with her mother.)*

WANDA. Hi, Aunt Ola Belle.

OLA BELLE. Hi, Sug.

WANDA. We're gonna have fun, aren't we, while Mama's gone?

OLA BELLE. We sure are.

WANDA. Can we go to the picture show?

OLA BELLE. I reckon so.

WANDA. And can we have a hamburger and french fries and ride around?

OLA BELLE. I don't see why not. And we might even play a few hands of rummy.

WANDA. Oh, goody! And we can work the Ouija board and find out some things.

OLA BELLE. Crap on that! I don't want to know what's

going to happen. I might not be able to stand it if I knew what was ahead.

FLORENE. *(puts last few items in her bag)* Well, I guess I'm ready, and nobody's going to miss me a bit. *(As she starts to close the bag, she picks up the letter which WANDA put in earlier.)* What's this?

WANDA. It's from me to Daddy about my singing lessons — in case he didn't get the other letter. *(sternly)* And you'd better give it to him, too!

FLORENE. *(thrusts it back at WANDA)* Give it to the postman. Or Althea Lockwood. Let her do whatever she wants to with it.

WANDA. *(desperate)* Mama, please make him let me take those lessons.

FLORENE. Wanda, this trip is not about you and that music teacher. It's about me and my husband. And we're fixing to set Wichita Falls on fire! *(closes suitcase)*

WANDA. Aunt Ola Belle, can I — may I — sit under the steering wheel coming back?

OLA BELLE. Well, maybe so.

FLORENE. Don't let her be driving, Ola Belle. It's too dangerous. *(As an afterthought, she opens suitcase again and removes map.)* Even I'm afraid to try it. Besides, she's still a child. *(closes suitcase)* Ya'll take care of things now.

OLA BELLE. We will. We will. *(WANDA puts on her houseshoes.)*

FLORENE. *(consulting map)* Texas is really big, isn't it? But I won't be very far from the Red River and Oklahoma. And look at all the rest of these states I've never seen. I guess Europe is too far away to even get on this map ... I'll miss you, Wanda.

OLA BELLE. *(Speaking for WANDA, who remains sullen and silent.)* We will you, too. We're going to eat our hearts out this week thinking about all the fun you're having up there.

FLORENE. I guess if he's not at his rooming house, they'll let me in to wait for him. Surely to goodness they will.

OLA BELLE. Quit worrying now.

FLORENE. Ya'll lissen to the radio today for bus wrecks. *(She waits for OLA BELLE to give her more words of encouragement, but she does not. FLORENE picks up her suitcase.)* Okay. Les go.

*(OLA BELLE takes FLORENE'S sack lunch, turns out lamp, and exits arm in arm with WANDA. FLORENE stops as she gets to the door and looks back at the house she is leaving. Then she exits decisively. Lights go down. End of Act I.)*

# ACT II

# Scene 1

*Two weeks later. Late afternoon. Lights up on Kings' side of house. OLA BELLE and WANDA enter from outside and go into Kings' living room.*

WANDA. Aunt Ola Belle, wasn't that *Daddy Long Legs* the best picture show you ever saw?
OLA BELLE. Naw. *I Am a Fugitive from a Chain Gang* is still at the top of my list.
WANDA. But it was so pretty, and the way they danced and everything.
OLA BELLE. That was nice — but not true to life. Even if you could believe that people who were not supposed to be dancers were able to dance that good, you know they couldn't just start right in to dance together. They'd have to at least take a minute to talk about what they knew how to do.
WANDA. That would spoil the story.
OLA BELLE. I don't know about that. I think it might be funny. *(acting)* "Would you care to dance? See, I can lift my leg about knee high and turn around once before I get dizzy. What can you do?"
WANDA. *(Laughing, but pulling herself together to act.)* "I can lift my leg up to my shoulder and whirl around forever." *(She sweeps around the room on her tiptoes, dragging OLA BELLE*

*with her.)* I bet I could be a dancer. I like the way he lifted her up in the air. She looked as light as a feather, didn't she?

OLA BELLE. She was, I expect. She's as pore as a old cow. *(Grabs flyswatter from radio and puts it under her arm as if it's a cane.)* I feel just like Fred Astaire.

WANDA. *(Still dancing with OLA BELLE.)* Aunt Ola Belle, I'm going to do something with my life. I know I can if I just try.

OLA BELLE. Well, Sug, I sure hope you can. That's what we all wanted to do at one time.

WANDA. Why didn't you then?

OLA BELLE. *(Winded, she puts flyswatter on radio and sits down.)* We tried. but it turned out to be harder than we thought it would.

WANDA. I'm not going to give up — ever. I'll be different and get what I want. What did you want to do?

OLA BELLE. Oh ... I wanted to be pretty and dainty like Florene was and have everybody make a fuss over me. But people would just look at me and say, "Boy, that Ola Belle is tough! She's big enough to go bear huntin' with a switch."

WANDA. Really? You wanted to be like Mama?

OLA BELLE. Yes. But if you ever tell that, Wanda, I'll deny it quicker than Peter did Christ at Gethsemane.

WANDA. I won't tell. I can keep a secret.

OLA BELLE. Yep. I used to wish I looked like her and could sing like she did too. Seemed like she had everything.

WANDA. I have a secret too — a secret from Mama.

OLA BELLE. What's that?

WANDA. Miz Lockwood's entered me in a talent contest.

OLA BELLE. That's nice. Why can't Florene know?

WANDA. She might not let me be in it. She hates Miz Lockwood and won't let me take singing lessons with her.

OLA BELLE. She may be right, Sug. You need to be learning something practical. I don't want you to walk around in a dream all your life like Florene. Learn some kind of business so you can be the boss someday.

WANDA. I don't want to be a boss. I want to be a singer.

OLA BELLE. So did Florene. Look where it got her.

WANDA. There's a $200 prize, Aunt Ola Belle. If I win it, I can afford to pay for my own lessons. Miz Lockwood says with my natural talent plus the vocal training and good grades to back me up, I'll have a chance of getting a music scholarship to college. That's what I want to do. But don't tell Mama. Okay?

*(Just then FLORENE races up onto the porch. She calls as she dashes into her living room.)*

FLORENE. King? King? I saw a blue Ford parked in front of our house.

OLA BELLE. That's what I'm driving till they get my car fixed. Besides, I thought he wasn't due until tomorrow.

FLORENE. His letter said probably tomorrow, but maybe tonight. I was just afraid he might have got here while I was gone. Those folks I was babysitting for were an hour late getting home.

OLA BELLE. It wouldn't hurt him to wait.

FLORENE. No ... But everybody else would get to see him first.

WANDA. You got to be with him in Wichita Falls. I haven't seen him since Christmas. I deserve to get to see him first. *(Still suffering from having been excluded from the Wichita Falls trip, her attitude toward her mother is resentful and accusatory.)*

OLA BELLE. Yeah, Florene. With the kind of visit you told us about, you ought to be able to let Wanda take her turn.

FLORENE. I will. I will.

WANDA. Mama, what was the name of that nightclub he took you to in Wichita Falls?

FLORENE. Uh ... I can't think of it right now.

WANDA. I'm surprised they let you in there without an evening dress.

FLORENE. Oh, they didn't. I mean, I had one.

WANDA. I haven't got to see it!

FLORENE. Oh, I borrowed it — from one of the other rassler's wives. She was just my size.

WANDA. What color was it?

FLORENE. Uh — kind of greenish purple.

WANDA. Sounds ugly.

FLORENE. No. It was gorgeous. It's just hard to describe. I had so much fun everything's run together in my mind.

OLA BELLE. Ya'll must've partied every minute. I tell you, you looked like a tree full of owls when you got back here. Didn't ya'll ever sleep?

FLORENE. No. Not much ... You know how that is.

OLA BELLE. Can't say I do. Well, I better shove off. I've got to get ready for work. *(Goes to screen door. FLORENE and WANDA follow her.)* Looks kind of dark over in the west.

FLORENE. Drive careful. Thanks for taking Wanda to the picture show.

WANDA. Thank you, Aunt Ola Belle. *(OLA BELLE exits.)*

FLORENE. How was the picture show?

WANDA. Good.

FLORENE. Aren't you going to tell me about it?

WANDA. No. Aunt Ola Belle and I had fun. We danced together.

FLORENE. Oh, isn't that nice? ... I sure did keep a sweet baby this afternoon. I sang her to sleep — like I used to sing to you when you were a baby.

WANDA. I'll be thirteen this time next year.

*(HATTIE, carrying half a pecan pie, appears in her USC doorway and exits onto porch. She heads toward Kings' door.)*

FLORENE. I know.

WANDA. Didn't Daddy say *anything* about my singing lessons?

FLORENE. Well, he — Wanda, he had other things on his mind. He said we'll have to wait and see what happens.

WANDA. What happens about what?

FLORENE. About everything, I guess. We were too busy having a good time to get that serious, Wanda.

*(HATTIE knocks at their door. FLORENE leaps to answer it.)*

FLORENE. This may be him! King? I need to talk — Oh, Miz Hattie. Come in. I thought you were my husband.

*(HATTIE enters.)*

HATTIE. You all ready for the tornado?
FLORENE. What tornado?
HATTIE. We're under a tornado alert till midnight. All the neighbors are leaving for the storm cellar. Ya'll can get a ride with somebody if you hurry.
FLORENE. Oh, I don't want to go off with my husband expected. Wanda, maybe you ought to go though.
WANDA. *(defiant)* No, I want to be here when Daddy comes. You just want him all to yourself.
FLORENE. That's not so. Aren't you going, Miz Hattie?
HATTIE. Naw. Cooking this pie wore me out. *(Hands pie to FLORENE.)*
FLORENE. Thank you, Miz Hattie.
HATTIE. I'm going to eat my supper and go to bed.
WANDA. Miz Hattie, it's not even six o'clock.
HATTIE. I'm not ruled by the clock. These old bones tell me what to do.
WANDA. What about Westinghouse Theatre? We were going to watch it at 8:00.
HATTIE. There won't be no t.v. here tonight. That television will draw down lightning quicker than you can say Jack Robinson. Ya'll eat that pie. It's made from pecans off that tree in the backyard. Yes'ir, I took the blue

ribbon ten years in a row at the county fair with this recipe.

FLORENE. Thank you, Miz Hattie. I know we'll enjoy it ... Tornadoes don't ever hit Sparta, do they? Waco and San Angelo are where they ususally come down.

HATTIE. A lot of folks in them towns have got blowed away.

WANDA. Were they bad people?

HATTIE. I wouldn't be surprised.

WANDA. Are we bad enough to get blown away?

HATTIE. Might be. Hosea 8:7: "For they have sown the wind and they shall reap the whirlwind." *(Exits, returning to her living room, where she exits offstage through her USC doorway.)*

FLORENE. Wanda, I think you ought to go to that storm cellar.

*(ETHYL enters onto porch and proceeds to Kings' door.)*

WANDA. No! *You* go. And let *me* wait for Daddy.

*(ETHYL knocks.)*

FLORENE. This is him. *(WANDA races her to the door, but FLORENE gets there ahead of her.)* Oh, Miz Ethyl. Hello. Come in.

ETHYL. *(enters)* I've just got a minute. I'm on my way to Dallas. Howdee, Wanda. My art teacher is taking us all to a art show.

FLORENE. Did you know we're under a tornado alert?

ETHYL. Tornado? No! Is Dallas too?

FLORENE. I think so. It looks like the storm is forming over in the west.

ETHYL. Good! We'll be driving toward it then. I'd sure hate to miss it. I think a tornado's kind of a spiral-looking do-dad. Maybe I could paint it. I expect to be able to paint you when I get back, Florene. So you be ready. *(glances out door looking for her ride)*

FLORENE. Wouldn't you rather paint Wanda? Look at that face. Not a line or a disappointment on it. *(WANDA scowls.)*

ETHYL. She's as cute as a bug. But I still want to show you, Florene. I just don't know how yet. But I will. Things are coming to me pretty quick ever since I took Ola Belle's advice.

FLORENE. *(shaking her head and smiling)* I hate to think what she told you to do.

ETHYL. Honey, she just told me to jump in and do something wild — without even thinking about it. So I've donated the old family farm place to my painting teacher to start a school here in Sparta — the Ethyl Roberts School of Art. I signed the deed today.

FLORENE. You did what?

*(A car horn sounds.)*

ETHYL. There's my ride. I have to run get my suitcase. I'm off to Dallas! *(exits.)*

FLORENE. Wanda, she's given away Ola Belle's farm!

WANDA. I know it.

FLORENE. Oh, poor Ola Belle! Just when things

seemed to be working out for her, too. That farm's all she's been living for ... I wish I could *do* something ... Well, I'll break it to her myself tomorrow. Les have some of Miz Hattie's prize-winning pie and pick up our spirits. *(Exits through USL doorway to kitchen. Calls from offstage.)* We don't want King to find us long-faced. *(She re-enters with a knife and napkins and cuts a piece for each of them.)* It looks good. *(They bite into their respective pieces and stop chewing about the same time.)* Are there hulls in yours?

WANDA. *(spitting)* Uh-huh.

FLORENE. Mine too. *(spits)* This is a pecan *hull* pie.

WANDA. Ugh!

FLORENE. *(still spitting out hulls)* Well, I guess Miz Hattie's eyes are just too bad to pick out nuts anymore. But she won't admit it. It's hard to outlive your blue ribbons, I expect ... We'll have to tell her we liked it. *(WANDA has gotten some bright red fingernail polish from dresser and is shaking it vigorously.)* What are you doing?

WANDA. Getting ready for Daddy.

FLORENE. *(checking her impulse to correct WANDA)* That's a bright color — but nice. I just bought it. Do you mind if I use some when you're done?

WANDA. No. *(WANDA paints her nails.)*

FLORENE. Do you want me to paint your right hand?

WANDA. No. I can do it. *(She messes up.)* Oh, shoot! I painted my finger.

FLORENE. Let me do that for you. You're going to waste all the polish. *(WANDA, smoldering, submits. FLORENE proceeds to paint WANDA'S nails. As she does so, she glances at a picture in an open Photoplay Magazine on the sofa.)* Wanda, now be honest. Does it seem like to you that I'm looking older?

WANDA. *(studying her seriously)* No. You look the same to me.

FLORENE. *(pointing to the magazine)* I want you to look at this picture of Loretta Young. Which one of us looks older? Tell the truth.

WANDA. *(Struggling between her impulse to be objective and truthful and her desire for revenge.)* Well — she sure is pretty. Look how her face is shaped.

FLORENE. Yes, she is. Always was. Who looks older though — her or me?

WANDA. Well, I guess ya'll look about the same.

FLORENE. I look as old as her?

WANDA. Except maybe you look younger. She might have false teeth.

FLORENE. *(looking closely)* I don't think so. So I look younger?

WANDA. Yeah. Yeah, you do.

FLORENE. How much?

WANDA. Oh, about a year, I guess.

*(There is a loud clap of thunder. WANDA jumps.)*

WANDA. Oooh!

FLORENE. *(glancing out)* I hope King gets ahead of that. It's really getting dark out there.

*(The lights have faded into the eerie, greenish cast of a pre-storm sky.)*

ACT II             THE ALTO PART             63

    FLORENE. Why won't you talk to me, Wanda?
    WANDA. I don't have anything to say.
    FLORENE. Don't be like this. Come on. Les have some fun. It's summer. *(turns on radio)* Our last summer before you're a teenager.

*(A sad, dreamy popular song plays, preferably something in a waltz tempo.)*

    FLORENE. Oh, I love that song. It's so sad and sweet. Dance with me.
    WANDA. I don't want to.
    FLORENE. You danced with Ola Belle. Come on. *(Pulls WANDA from her chair.)* We used to have such good times together. *(Leads her around the room in a stumbling waltz.)*
    WANDA. *(She is a surly, reluctant partner.)* I can't tell where you're going, Mama.
    FLORENE. I'm doing the best I can, Wanda. I'm not used to doing the man's part ... I think I'm the same age as Loretta Young, but I thought I looked a whole lot younger.

*(They continue to dance to the song. The sky darkens and the wind gets up. A bolt of lightning nearby knocks out the radio.)*

    WANDA. What happened?

*(HATTIE emerges from her USC doorway and goes to telephone. She picks it up and tries to dial, but apparently it is dead. She takes her Bible from the telephone table and sits in rocking chair.)*

FLORENE. I guess that lightning blew out a tube. *(adjusts radio dial, trying to tune it in)*
WANDA. I'm scared.
FLORENE. Well, now, don't be. I expect King to drive up any minute.

*(There is more lightning and thunder and increasing wind. WANDA bounds across the floor to look out the door.)*

FLORENE. Careful, Wanda. Remember these shaky floors.
WANDA. *(becoming panicky)* We're not nailed down to anything, are we? Aunt Ola Belle's always saying how a strong gust of wind will blow us off these building blocks.
FLORENE. *(Trying to hide her fear of their precarious predicament, which has now dawned on her.)* Now, Wanda, calm down. *(WANDA frantically grabs a large envelope from the top of the radio and clutches it to her chest. FLORENE points to the envelope.)* What is that?

*(More lightning and thunder. WANDA'S hysteria mounts.)*

WANDA. None of your business.
FLORENE. Don't you sass me even if it is coming a tornado.
WANDA. I want my Daddy.
FLORENE. Maybe we ought not to wait for him. I'm going to call Miz Hattie. *(beats on wall)* Miz Hattie? Miz Hattie! That storm is looking bad!
HATTIE. *(calling back)* Don't I know it? I'm setting here

reading my Bible and watching it.

FLORENE. Don't you think we ought to telephone somebody to come carry us to a storm cellar?

HATTIE. It's too late for that. Everybody's done gone. There's not a car left on the block. Besides, the telephone's dead as a hammer. I expect the wind knocked down some lines.

FLORENE. What will we do?

HATTIE. Not a thing, I reckon.

*(More lightning and thunder. Gusts of wind.)*

WANDA. Mama, I'm scared. *(She is crying.)*

FLORENE. I'll ask Miz Hattie to come over here and stay with us till this is over. She's not afraid of anything. *(calling)* Miz Hattie, I think it would be a good idea for us all to be together till this storm passes. Why don't you come over here?

HATTIE. I can't.

FLORENE. Why not?

HATTIE. I'm having a spell with my heart. I can't even get up out of my chair.

FLORENE. Oh, no! *(to WANDA)* What'll we do? Come on. I guess we have to go help her. *(WANDA cowers behind FLORENE, clutching her envelope, as they exit from their side of house.)* What *is* that you're hanging onto? *(They go up steps.)*

WANDA. I can't tell you. *(They enter HATTIE'S side of the house. She is sitting in rocking chair clutching her heart and gasping for breath.)*

FLORENE. *(shocked by HATTIE'S grave appearance)* Miz

Hattie! Can I do anything?

HATTIE. Get me some water and hand me them pills on the dresser. *(FLORENE exits hurriedly through USC doorway.)*

WANDA. Are you going to die, Miz Hattie?

HATTIE. Yes. And so are you — sooner or later. *(FLORENE returns with water and administers the pills.)*

FLORENE. You need a doctor.

HATTIE. These pills will help ... I just can't breathe. *(FLORENE gets a paper fan and begins to fan her.)* That's better. It's easing up some now.

*(More lightning and thunder. WANDA goes to SR foyer window to look out, still clutching her envelope.)*

HATTIE. Wanda, you better get away from that window.

WANDA. *(does not move)* I'm watching for my daddy.

HATTIE. You mind me. That wind'll suck you out and carry you all the way to Louisiana.

WANDA. *(Scared, moves back, crying.)* I don't want to die.

FLORENE. *(still fanning HATTIE)* Nobody does. Now stay over here, and calm down. See how brave Miz Hattie is?

WANDA. It's easy for her to be brave. She's old and already had her life. I haven't even started to live yet.

FLORENE. I haven't either. Not really.

WANDA. You have too. You've been to Galveston and Wichita Falls and had cocktails at nightclubs.

HATTIE. Cocktails at nightclubs? The Lord have mercy! Don't stand so close to me, Florene! I better get to reading this Bible. *(She starts searching the scriptures.)*

FLORENE. Well, now it wasn't like it sounds, Miz Hattie.

WANDA. And you've had a chance to sing.

FLORENE. I never had a chance to sing!

WANDA. Yes, you did! You just didn't do it!

FLORENE. The only time I ever got to sing was at that nightclub in Galveston.

*(Lightning, thunder, and wind.)*

HATTIE. Nightclub again. *(reading from Bible)* "They that plow iniquity, and sow wickedness, reap the same."

FLORENE. That was a long time ago, Miz Hattie. A long time ago.

WANDA. And you've been grown-up and in love and had Daddy.

FLORENE. Not enough.

WANDA. But you did in Wichita Falls! *(She has moved back closer to window.)*

HATTIE. You better get away from that window, Young Lady.

FLORENE. *(Jerks WANDA back from the window.)* Get back here, Wanda. Stand behind me, and don't you move till this is over!

WANDA. Why? So you can see him first when he drives up?

*(Defiantly goes back to window. FLORENE yanks her away. The wind howls.)*

FLORENE. What's wrong with you? Do you want to die?

*(A bolt of lightning followed by a strong clap of thunder.)*

WANDA. *(hysterical)* I won't ever get to see him! And I won't get to be in that talent contest. I'll die before I ever get to do anything!
FLORENE. What talent contest?
WANDA. The one Miz Lockwood entered me in.
FLORENE. She has no right slipping around behind my back entering you in contests.
WANDA. She does so! She paid my entrance fee, and she's coaching me for free for the contest. *(indicating the envelope she is holding)* She even bought me this sheet music I'm going to sing.

*(More lightning, thunder, and wind.)*

WANDA. And now I'll die before I get to do it! I missed Galveston, and I missed Wichita Falls! When is it my turn?
HATTIE. This ain't helping my heart. I can tell you that.
FLORENE. Oh, Wanda, you've got it all wrong. Galveston was too long ago to hold against me. Besides, I don't know if I even remember it the way it actually happened. And Wichita Falls — well, Wichita Falls wasn't like you think it was.
WANDA. Yes, it was! You got to go! You went!

ACT II  THE ALTO PART  69

*(Increasing storm sounds.)*

FLORENE. I went! Yes, I went — on a wild goose chase! I never even got to see your daddy. He had already left for Abilene when I got there. I spent two days and nights sitting up in the bus station because I was too ashamed to come back and look like a fool in front of you and Althea Lockwood and everybody else. I made it all up, Wanda! Every bit of it! Now, do you feel better?

*(There is a sharp gust of wind and the sound of timber falling, windows breaking, etc.)*

FLORENE. Part of a roof just blew away.
WANDA. We're not even nailed down!
FLORENE. There goes your pecan tree, Miz Hattie.

*(A loud roaring commences.)*

WANDA. What is that?
FLORENE. It's a twister!

*(She grabs WANDA to her. The roaring continues for a moment and then dies down until it is perfectly quiet.)*

WANDA. It's over. It's over, isn't it?
FLORENE. *(Looking up to accept whatever is coming.)* I don't know. Sometimes it's the quietest before the storm hits. *(blackout)*

# Scene 2

*Three days later. Mid-to-late afternoon. Lights up on porch. HATTIE is sitting in glider. FLORENE enters from outside. She wears a black dress and hat and carries a black purse, a paper fan, and a handkerchief. She has acquired a new solemnity, appearing sad, but tranquil. HATTIE stops her before she gets to her door.*

HATTIE. How was the funeral?

FLORENE. Sad. Real sad.

HATTIE. I sure did hate it that I had to miss it.

FLORENE. Nobody expected you to go, Miz Hattie. Everybody knows you've been sick.

HATTIE. Yes, but I try to go to all the funerals I can. If you don't go to other people's, they won't come to yours.

FLORENE. Who would have thought such a thing could happen? Just swept away! They were so young and innocent! It wasn't anytime ago that Wanda and I set out here and watched them come back from their honeymoon.

HATTIE. Did they lay 'em away nice?

FLORENE. Oh, yes.

HATTIE. Was they lots of flowers?

FLORENE. Too many to fit into the church house.

HATTIE. How was the music?

FLORENE. Good, I hope. *(sits in glider with HATTIE)* I sang.

HATTIE. Well, do tell. I hope you didn't sing "Pearly White City." That has been wore to a nub.

FLORENE. No, ma'am, I didn't ... Some lady there asked me to sing at her daughter's wedding next month. So I think I did all right.

HATTIE. Did you take a dish for the family?

FLORENE. Yes, ma'am. Deviled eggs and green beans.

HATTIE. If I'd felt better, I'd have made a pecan pie.

FLORENE. I wouldn't worry about it. There was plenty of food.

HATTIE. What scripture was read?

FLORENE. The twenty-third Psalm.

HATTIE. That's good.

FLORENE. I've always liked it. But you know what bothers me about it, Miz Hattie — not only that Psalm — but the whole idea of salvation, I guess? What bothers me is the thought of just having to be one of the flock.

HATTIE. They say a shepherd knows every one of his sheep.

FLORENE. But that's still being one of many. I always wanted to stand out.

HATTIE. It's good you wasn't a sheep then, Florene. The wolves would probably have eat you ... Ola Belle came by and took Wanda to her lesson.

FLORENE. Yes, ma'am. I know.

HATTIE. I'm surprised ya'll can afford singing lessons. I have to dun you to get the rent.

FLORENE. Ola Belle's paying for Wanda's lessons. This is her first one.

HATTIE. I bet Ola Belle was fit to be tied when she

found out about Ethyl's farm.

FLORENE. She was awful let down. I never saw her so low. But she rallied. As soon as I told her Wanda was counting on her — needed her help for those lessons — she came up fighting.

HATTIE. Humph. What's happened to Mr. King? I thought he was supposed to be here three days ago.

FLORENE. He was. But he got delayed. I don't know when he'll be here now. I guess I'll look for him when I see him coming.

HATTIE. I want to see him. *(Rises from glider and starts up steps to her side of house.)* I'm starting to think ya'll made him up.

FLORENE. Seems like it, doesn't it, Miz Hattie? ... *(to herself)* I guess I'll sing "Always" for that wedding.

*(Lights go down.)*

# Scene 3

*Two days later. 3:00 a.m. Lights up on HATTIE'S side of house as her telephone rings. After a few rings she stumbles into the living room from USC doorway to answer it, muttering to herself.*

HATTIE. Who in the world is calling me in the middle of the night? *(picks up receiver)* Hello? ... What? ... I can't understand a word you're saying ... Are you talking

English? ... Florene King? Is that what you said? ... Well, you better learn how to talk. Yes, she's here ... I mean, I'll have to call her to the phone. You wait a minute. *(She puts down receiver.)* The Lord have mercy! *(Beats on wall and calls into FLORENE'S side of house.)* Florene? Florene! Come to the telephone!

*(Lights up on Kings' living room, where WANDA is sleeping.)*

FLORENE. *(calling from offstage)* What? What is it?
HATTIE. *(beating on wall and yelling)* They's a Mexican calling you long distance at 3:00 o'clock in the morning on my telephone. Get in here!

*(FLORENE emerges from USL door fastening her robe.)*

FLORENE. Yes, ma'am. I'm coming! Oh, my goodness!
WANDA. *(who has been awakened by the commotion)* Mama, what is it?
FLORENE. A long distance phone call. *(She exits hastily, goes up steps, and enters HATTIE'S living room.)*
HATTIE. I didn't know you knew any foreigners.
FLORENE. I don't. *(She approaches the telephone warily, but with less panic than she showed in Act I, Scene 1 when King called.)* Hello? ... Yes, this is her ... King? King, is that you? ... Are you all right? ... You sound awful far away. And what's that music I hear? ... What kind of fiesta? ... What are you doing in Mexico?

*(WANDA enters in her nightgown. FLORENE still keeps talking*

*to King, but her conversation becomes inaudible to the audience as HATTIE and WANDA speak to each other. In their silences, her conversation once again is heard.)*

WANDA. Who is it?

HATTIE. It's your daddy and some Mexicans.

WANDA. Daddy? Mama, let me talk.

FLORENE. In a minute, Wanda. I promise. *(to telephone)* Well, it's just wonderful to hear your voice ... An adventure?

HATTIE. Sounded like a bunch of drunk people whooping and hollering in the background.

WANDA. My daddy doesn't get drunk.

FLORENE. *(to HATTIE and WANDA)* This is a real bad connection, and I can barely hear him. Would ya'll mind going somewhere else to talk?

HATTIE. Don't that take the cake? Run out of my own house. Come on, Wanda. *(She starts to exit to porch. WANDA balks at having to leave the conversation, but FLORENE motions for her to go.)* You hurry up, Florene, and let me get back to bed. *(FLORENE resumes her telephone conversation as they exit onto porch.)*

FLORENE. A lot's been happening to me, too. And I've managed ... No, you would have been proud of the way I acted. *I* was ... *(HATTIE and WANDA sit in glider. WANDA is furious at having been barred from the telephone call. She tries to listen from the porch and absentmindedly begins to swing.)*

HATTIE. Your daddy has hisself a high-heeled time, don't he?

WANDA. He's fun.

FLORENE. Well, sure I need you ... Of course it would be nice to have somebody to lean on.

HATTIE. You're going to have to cut out that swinging, Wanda. It makes me dizzy-headed.

WANDA. I don't know what anybody wants with a swing if they're not going to swing in it.

HATTIE. You will when you're my age.

WANDA. I don't intend to let myself get old.

HATTIE. I didn't either. Now quit moving this swing.

FLORENE. In the middle of the night? It seems so crazy.

WANDA. I can sing, but Daddy doesn't know it yet. You want to hear me?

HATTIE. No. I want ya'll to go home and let me go to sleep. Besides, you better not be singing at night. "If you go to bed singing, you'll wake up crying." That's what I was always told.

WANDA. *(Gets out of glider, runs up steps, and opens screen door.)* Is it my turn yet?

FLORENE. Not yet. I'll call you.

WANDA. *(Disgusted, she closes the door and stands with her back to it.)* I always have to be second.

FLORENE. *(Resumes her conversation with King. She is giddy, high with excitement.)* I *am* excited ... Right now? ... I feel too silly ... Oh, all right. *(She overcomes her embarrassment and begins to sing softly.)*

MAYBE YOU'LL THINK OF ME,
WHEN YOU ARE ALL ALONE,15

*(WANDA, who has turned around at screen door to face her, chimes in, singing loud enough to be heard by her father, she hopes. She tries to drown out FLORENE.)*

FLORENE and WANDA.
MAYBE THE ONE WHO IS WAITING FOR YOU

WILL PROVE UNTRUE
THEN WHAT WILL YOU DO.16
*(FLORENE stops singing.)*

FLORENE. Wanda, sssh. Not so loud. *(back to phone)* That's enough, King ... I'm glad you liked it ... King, I want you to talk to Wanda now. You wouldn't know her. *(Motions for WANDA to come inside.)* She's going to be as excited as I am ... All right. I can't wait. Here's Wanda. *(Hands receiver to WANDA.)*

WANDA. Hi Daddy! *(to FLORENE)* You wait out there now, Mama. *(FLORENE exits to porch.)* I'm going to sing in a talent contest and win some money for singing lessons and scholarships and things ... I'm going to college ... But what about school?

FLORENE. Sorry for the bother, Miz Hattie. *(There is about her a feeling of secrecy, urgency, and excitement.)*

HATTIE. What does he mean a'callin' at this hour?

FLORENE. I guess it's not so late there.

HATTIE. I heard some senoritas in the background. They was awful tickled about something.

FLORENE. It's a fiesta. Everybody's having a good time. *(She is rankled.)*

HATTIE. I bet.

WANDA. I know how to have a good time ... Yes'ir, I could do that.

HATTIE. When's he coming?

FLORENE. *(evasive)* Uh, not for a while.

HATTIE. He ain't ready to say adios to them senoritas.

WANDA. What kind of presents? ... Are mine as good as Mama's?

HATTIE. No, sir. He just ain't ready to say adios.

FLORENE. *(furious)* The honeysuckle sure smells sweet at this time of night. It's the first time I ever set out here so late to enjoy it.

HATTIE. It better be the last time, too.

FLORENE. *(signigicantly)* It will be.

WANDA. Yes'ir. Yes'ir. I'm brave enough ... Bye! Bye, Daddy! *(She hangs up and rushes out onto the porch, spilling over with excitement.)* Mama, we're—

FLORENE. *(Interrupting her before she reveals too much.)* Les say good night, Wanda, and let Miz Hattie get back to bed. Thank you, ma'am. Hope we didn't disturb you too much.

HATTIE. *(rising from glider)* If I'm a corpse tomorrow, you can take the credit. *(She goes back into her side of the house and exits through her USC door.)*

FLORENE. I have never known such a hateful person.

WANDA. Mama, we're going! We're going with him! *(They enter their living room.)*

FLORENE. We sure are. Just think — we'll be meeting him this very afternoon in San Antonio! It seems like a dream. But we have to hurry. We've got less than an hour to catch the bus. *(WANDA exits through USL doorway. FLORENE checks her wallet.)* Thank goodness for my ironing and babysitting money. I've got plenty for our tickets. *(WANDA re-enters carrying two suitcases.)* Just pack the things you absolutely can't do without. Don't take too many clothes. He's going to buy us some new ones. *(They start hurriedly getting clothes out of closet and the dresser drawers.)*

WANDA. Where'd he get all that money?

FLORENE. Same place he got the trailer house.

WANDA. What trailer house?

FLORENE. Oh, he didn't tell you about that? He won it in a poker game in Old Mexico. That's where we'll live while we're on the road. He's really on a streak of luck. This new rasslin' circuit out West just fell into his lap at the last minute. He's going all the way to California with it. Think about that, Wanda! And we're going with him!

WANDA. He has presents for us, too. And we're both getting the same things. He told me so. I'm getting grown-up presents.

FLORENE. Isn't that nice? We're going to see the world. Lots of new places. And I won't ever have to iron or babysit again. And we won't have to put up with Miz Hattie anymore. We're going to leave all our troubles behind us... *(chuckles to herself)* Made me sing to him long distance! *(glances at clock)* We better step on it. How are you coming with your packing?

WANDA. Okay. But it's hard to decide what to take and what to leave.

FLORENE. I know. It seems awful just to move off in the middle of the night and leave all our stuff. But this is what we've been waiting for. And there's not time to do anything else. It'll serve Miz Hattie right in a way. *(exits through USL doorway)*

WANDA. She said Daddy was drunk.

FLORENE. *(offstage)* She just can't stand to see anybody enjoy themselves.

WANDA. *(at closet)* I'm not packing any of these school dresses. Okay?

FLORENE. *(Re-enters through USL doorway wearing a slip.)*

Okay ... I wonder what Miz Hattie will do with the stuff we leave ... I wish she'd give it to those people who lost things in the storm. Well, we lived through it, didn't we, Wanda? We can always tell people we survived the Sparta tornado.

WANDA. I wasn't even scared.

FLORENE. I don't think King believed how well I took care of things. Or that I made a trip all by myself to Wichita Falls. Shoot. I believe I could go to Timbuktu now if I had to.

WANDA. Everybody will wonder and wonder what happened to us.

FLORENE. That's true. I better leave a note for Ola Belle so she won't think we got kidnapped. *(With difficulty she composes a note.)*

WANDA. Daddy doesn't want me to end up like her.

FLORENE. *(Surprised at WANDA'S attitude.)* Don't you be critical of Ola Belle, Wanda. She's been true-blue to you. To both us us.

WANDA. Miz Hattie's going to be surprised when she wakes up tomorrow and finds us gone. She'll have to watch her t.v. without us tomorrow night.

FLORENE. *(pinning note to screen door)* Yes, she will. I've learned to tolerate her a lot better than I ever thought I could. Sometimes I think she kindly likes us. *(She crosses to coffee table and searches under magazines on it.)* Where's that recipe for pecan pie she gave me? Here it is. *(Puts it in her purse.)* I'm going to take it with me. Without the hulls, I bet it would be real good ... I hope she'll be all right alone and her with that heart condition. I think the real reason she let us rent this place so cheap was because she knew she was in bad shape and she was afraid to be here without anybody.

WANDA. We'll never get to know if the Ouija board was right.

FLORENE. Right about what?

WANDA. When Miz Hattie dies.

FLORENE. No. *(Goes to closet to get more of her clothes and notices WANDA'S school dresses.)* Wanda, what about these school dresses?

WANDA. I told you I'm not taking them. I won't be going to school any more to wear them.

FLORENE. *(puzzled)* Well, now you're going to have to go to school somewhere. But we don't have to worry about that till September. *(She starts packing the dresses.)*

WANDA. No, I don't. I don't need to, Daddy said. *(She takes back the dresses and proceeds to hang them in closet.)* I'm going to get a different kind of education — a education in life. I won't have to waste my time stuck in a little shitheel school reading about things in books because I'll be doing it all firsthand. Life's a adventure, Mama — that's what Daddy said. You're supposed to enjoy yourself every minute and have fun. But most people are scared to.

FLORENE. *(She is stunned by this espousal of King's credo. However, she continues packing and getting ready.)* That's sure been his philosophy.

WANDA. We can go to all the rasslin' matches with Daddy, can't we?

FLORENE. Yes — yes, we can, if we want to.

WANDA. And Daddy said we'll sing at some nightclubs on the road.

FLORENE. What about Althea Lockwood? And that contest?

WANDA. I don't need to be in it anymore. I can sing to Daddy ... She was making me sing a bunch of boring old scales anyway. *(looks at clock)* We've got to hurry. I'm going to get dressed. *(She exits through USL doorway and can be heard singing.)*

MAYBE YOU'LL THINK OF ME,
WHEN YOU ARE ALL ALONE...17
*(FLORENE is left alone to finish her packing. She is disturbed. She comes across WANDA'S envelope of music for the contest and lays it aside. WANDA enters in organdy dress from Act I, Scene 1. She is carrying a pair of her mother's stockings.)*

WANDA. I'm borrowing these. My legs have filled out lately. *(She puts the stockings in her suitcase.)* You better hurry, Mama. We haven't got long. I'm nearly ready.

FLORENE. *(Picking up the envelope of music and handing it to WANDA.)* Here. You forgot to pack this.

WANDA. *(She is in conflict. Finally she pitches it on the radio.)* I don't need it anymore. I was getting tired of it. I'd rather be with Daddy.

FLORENE. What about your plans for college?

WANDA. I can't let anything rule my life. Not even singing. That's what Daddy said ... And I told you, we'll sing on the road. What color are the lights, Mama?

FLORENE. What?

WANDA. The lights in a nightclub. Are they blue or red or what?

FLORENE. I don't remember. Different colors I guess. *(putting on stockings)*

WANDA. I wonder which songs Daddy should tell the

band to play for us. Well, his song first and then maybe "Deep Purple." Or else, "You're My Thrill." Oh, I know — "That Ole Devil Called Love." That would be good, wouldn't it, Mama?

FLORENE. No. No, I don't think so.

WANDA. Why not?

FLORENE. No band now would know those songs. They're too old.

WANDA. Couldn't we get the sheet music? You better hurry up, Mama, and get dressed.

FLORENE. I am. I am. I am.

WANDA. Daddy will just buy us the sheet music for the band then.

FLORENE. I doubt if bands would play that music, Wanda, even if they had it before them. Nobody wants to hear those old songs any more.

WANDA. Why not? They're pretty.

FLORENE. Yes. But they're out of date. Part of another time.

WANDA. We'll sing so good we'll bring that time back, Mama.

FLORENE. No, I think it's over. Over for good, Wanda.

WANDA. No. I won't let it be. I'll bring it back. I know all about it.

FLORENE. You don't know half of it. There are some things I don't even tell you, Wanda.

WANDA. Well, I'll find out from Daddy. He'll tell me. You better hurry up and get your dress on. It's nearly time for the bus.

FLORENE. Yes. *(She slips the Act I, Scene 1 dress — the one for*

*King's arrival — over her head and tries to fasten it. She struggles with the zipper, becoming more and more agitated.)*

WANDA. Here, let me fasten it. *(She moves to help her mother.)*

FLORENE. No. No, Wanda. I said no! *(Still struggling with the zipper.)* I can't make it — can't get it to — Don't you see? We can't go!

WANDA. *(She is shocked and frightened by her mother's anger.)* Mama—

FLORENE. Oh, Wanda, I'm sorry. Come here. I have to talk to you.

WANDA. No. We've got to get ready.

FLORENE. Wanda, you have to listen to me now.

WANDA. No. *(She is frantic now.)* We don't have time. I'm getting you ready. *(She tries to dress FLORENE.)*

FLORENE. I said we can't go.

WANDA. He's meeting our bus in San Antonio.

FLORENE. We won't be on it, Wanda.

WANDA. It's what we've been waiting for. He wants us to.

FLORENE. I don't care what he wants! That's not enough of a reason ... I'm sorry, Wanda. We can't live that way.

WANDA. I can. I can live any ole way as long as I can be with Daddy. It's what we dreamed about, Mama!

FLORENE. It's what *I* dreamed about. Me — not you! You don't even know yet what you want. But you deserve a chance to find out.

WANDA. I do! I do too know! You're the one who doesn't know anything. You don't even know how to love anybody! I bet you never loved him!

FLORENE. Don't you ever say that! Ever! I'll always love him. There are some things you don't understand, Wanda.

WANDA. I understand everything, and I love him more!

FLORENE. Maybe so. Maybe you do. But I love him in a different way. There will never be anybody else in my life like your daddy, Wanda. Don't say I never loved him. Don't try to take away from me what was mine.

WANDA. Mama, if you care about him, come on. Please!

FLORENE. I can't. I care more about us.

WANDA. That doesn't make any sense.

FLORENE. It will some day. You can feel two ways at the same time, Wanda. That's what makes life so hard.

WANDA. *(She is still unable to understand, but realizes that her mother cannot be dissuaded.)* I don't feel but one way. *(She closes her suitcase.)* I'll go without you. I can! *(She grabs her suitcase and starts toward the door. FLORENE steps in front of her.)* Let me by!

FLORENE. You're not going, Wanda.

WANDA. Get out of my way! You're too scared to go with him, but I'm not. And you can't stop me! *(She tries to get by her mother.)*

FLORENE. I love you enough to try. *(WANDA fights ferociously.)* I can hold you here till that bus leaves. And I will! *(WANDA fights as hard as she can, but FLORENE is larger and stronger. She pulls WANDA away from the door and flings her to the sofa, pinning her there with her own body.)*

WANDA. Let me go! Mama, let me go!

FLORENE. I love you, Wanda. Do you hear me?

WANDA. *(Struggles until she realizes she is whipped. Then she starts to cry.)* Mama, I'm missin' it! I'm missin' it! And it's your fault! I hate you! Hate you!

*(Lights go down.)*

# Scene 4

*A late afternoon in August two months later. WANDA is heard singing scales from the Kings' side of the house, although she is unseen. HATTIE enters porch area from outside wearing a sunbonnet. She stops to rest and fan herself. Just then her telephone rings. She laboriously climbs the steps to her side of the house. She is breathing heavily as she enters and picks up the receiver.*

HATTIE. Hello? ... Who? ... Wait a minute. I'll have to call her. *(calls)* Wanda, somebody's calling you on my telephone!

*(WANDA races out of their side of the house, slamming the screen door behind her, and bounds into HATTIE'S living room, slamming screen door.)*

WANDA. Thank you, Miz Hattie. I hope it wasn't any trouble.
HATTIE. I had to run up the steps to answer it. Like to

killed myself.

WANDA. I sure am sorry. *(HATTIE exits to porch, where she will sit in glider. WANDA picks up receiver.)* Hello? ... Miz Lockwood, what a surprise! I was just getting ready to come for my lesson ... You can't? Why not? ... Oh, no! How did that happen? ... Well, what about the piano in the music hall at school? Couldn't we use that? ... Oh, I see ... *(Just then her eyes light on HATTIE'S piano.)* Miz Lockwood, I just thought of something. Could you come over here? Miz Hattie's got a piano. I bet she'd let us have my lesson on it just this once ... I'll see. Wait a minute.

*(Puts down receiver and runs out onto porch, slamming screen door behind her.)*

WANDA. Miz Hattie, somebody broke Miz Lockwood's piano, and she doesn't have a key to get in to use the one at school. And I was supposed to have my voice lesson today. So I wondered if maybe we could use your piano for it just this one time? It would only take thiry minutes.

HATTIE. That was Buddy Boy's piano. It hasn't been played since he left to go to war.

WANDA. I bet it still works though. And we'd be real careful with it.

HATTIE. I don't like the idea of that woman playing Buddy Boy's piano.

WANDA. Miz Hattie, please. It's covered with dust a inch thick. It needs to be used.

HATTIE. Well, I don't know, Wanda.

WANDA. Please, Miz Hattie. I'll die if I don't get to have

this lesson. I've been practicing for it all week.

HATTIE. Lord, you remind me of Buddy Boy. He said he'd die if I didn't buy him that piano, and I bought it for him, and he died anyway. Go on. Tell her yes. But ya'll better be done by my supper time.

WANDA. We will! We will! Oh, thank you, Miz Hattie!

*(Rushes back into HATTIE'S living room, slamming screen door behind her.)*

WANDA. She said yes, Miz Lockwood, if you'll come right on over before her supper time ... Okay, I'll see you. Bye.

*(Dashes out of HATTIE'S side of the house, slamming screen door behind her.)*

WANDA. Thank you, Miz Hattie.

*(Slams screen door behind her as she enters their side of house and disappears through their USL doorway. She flies back out with dust rag and grabs her envelope of sheet music from top of radio before exiting through screen door and slamming it behind her.)*

WANDA. I'm gonna shine it up real good, Miz Hattie.

*(Goes into HATTIE'S living room, slamming screen door behind her. She sings scales as she works on the piano.)*

HATTIE. I bet they's not a screen door left with a spring that still works.

*(Squealing tires, a car motor, and slamming car doors are heard. OLA BELLE and FLORENE enter in white uniforms.)*

HATTIE. Well, if it ain't the crew from the nut house. I'm surprised they let you out at night.
FLORENE. Hello, Miz Hattie.
OLA BELLE. Howdy-do.
HATTIE. Ya'll are late today.
FLORENE. That's my fault. I was trying to drive.
OLA BELLE. We followed a tractor all the way from Myrtle Springs. Florene was afraid to pass it.
FLORENE. It makes me nervous. I wasn't cut out to be a driver, and that's that!
OLA BELLE. All you need's some more practice.
FLORENE. That wouldn't help. It's just too hard for me.
OLA BELLE. I thought you was planning to take yourself some places and see the world.
FLORENE. I'll have to go on the bus — or stay at home. Because I cannot drive! *(She is upset. OLA BELLE changes the subject.)*
OLA BELLE. I believe we can thank Beelzebub for this hot spell. *(fanning her dress tail)* And we've still got some summer left.
HATTIE. It's hotter than rip in the house, but they's a good little breeze blowing out here. Take a load off your feet. *(FLORENE sits in chair; OLA BELLE sits in glider with HATTIE. She has to move HATTIE'S sunbonnet to do so.)*

FLORENE. Miz Hattie, have you been working out in the yard in this heat?

HATTIE. I was planting something. *(Looking around for something she has lost.)* Hummh. I must have left my watering can out there. I better go get it before it melts. *(Rises, puts on sunnbonnet, and exits to outside.)*

OLA BELLE. Wonder what she planted? Bitterweeds?

FLORENE. *(laughs)* Now, she's not that bad. Remember, she carried me on faith for the rent till I got a job. And it was *her* idea to do it. Wanda's spent a lot of the summer in there watching t.v. with her. Miz Hattie sees more of her than I do ... I guess Wanda's not ever going to forgive me.

OLA BELLE. She'll get over it after a while.

FLORENE. It's been two months now, and she still treats me like I'm her worst enemy. Wouldn't even let me go to hear her sing in that contest.

OLA BELLE. I thought she was the best damned one. And she should have had the first prize!

FLORENE. That money sure would have been nice for her, but I don't think she should feel too bad about second place. They gave her a medal with her name on it.

OLA BELLE. She's bounced back anyway. Already working on another scheme to make money for her music. I think she'll do all right with them Christmas cards, don't you?

FLORENE. What Christmas cards?

OLA BELLE. Oh, I thought you knew. She's taking orders from people for Christmas cards that they can get their names printed on. Real fancy. Something she wrote off for. I staked her for the samples.

FLORENE. *(Hurt that she's been excluded, but also proud of WANDA.)* She has a lot of ambition. I'm glad ... I hope she won't cut me entirely out of her life.

OLA BELLE. You going to be all right, Florene?

FLORENE. Yes ... I guess. Oh, I don't know! Sometimes I wonder if I haven't jumped off the deep end like Miz Ethyl did with her art school ... One of the inmates on my ward, somebody I thought liked me, threw a shoe at me this afternoon and hit me right on the ear. And for no reason.

OLA BELLE. Oh, she had a reason. It just wasn't one you could understand. You have to learn not to take it all so personal.

FLORENE. That's easy for some people.

*(HATTIE and ETHYL enter from outside. HATTIE has her watering can. ETHYL is extremely excited.)*

HATTIE. You better calm down, Ethyl. You're as red in the face as a turkey gobbler.

ETHYL. But it was so exciting, Hattie! And I saw the whole thing. Just let me tell you! *(She sees OLA BELLE and is aghast.)* Oh, I didn't know you were here, Ola Belle.

HATTIE. *(to OLA BELLE)* She's been hiding out from you all summer. *(She sits in glider.)*

ETHYL. Hattie!

HATTIE. She's afraid of what you're going to do to her for giving that farm away.

ETHYL. Nothing she could do would make me feel any worse than I already feel. And to think I donated my farm for a silly school of modern art. He wants us to paint so you can't recognize a thing.

OLA BELLE. What possessed you to do something so stupid? If you'd just stopped to think.

ETHYL. You told me not to, Honey. You said if I wanted to be wild not to think about anything.

OLA BELLE. You mean to tell me I put that notion in your head the night we set out here and drank that beer? *(ETHYL'S eyes widen at the mention of beer.)*

HATTIE. What beer?

OLA BELLE. Cokes. That's what I meant to say. Looks like I'd learn to keep my big mouth shut.

ETHYL. Can you ever forgive me?

OLA BELLE. Hell, yes.

HATTIE. Watch that cussing, Ola Belle.

OLA BELLE. Heck, yes, I meant. It's probably worked out for the best after all.

ETHYL. Phew! God bless you, Honey. Now, would anybody like to hear a secret about something exciting?

HATTIE. We better let her tell this. She's going to pop if we don't.

OLA BELLE. I'd sure like to hear a secret.

ETHYL. This secret is about love and romance. And it happened right here in Sparta.

FLORENE. I'd love to hear a story about romance, Miz Ethyl. *(wistfully)* I used to believe in it.

ETHYL. Well, I still do. And I witnessed this with my own eyes. It was *so* thrilling! *(WANDA, still polishing HATTIE'S piano, sings a few scales.)*

WANDA.
DO, ME SOL, DO, SOL, ME DO.

FLORENE. That's Wanda! What's she doing in your house, Miz Hattie?

HATTIE. She's in there shining up the piano. She talked me into letting her have that music teacher give her a singing lesson on it.

ETHYL. *(drawing in her breath)* She's the one I'm trying to tell about.

HATTIE. Who?

*(WANDA exits from HATTIE'S living room and comes down steps.)*

ETHYL. That music teacher, Althea Lockwood.

WANDA. *(on porch now)* Hi, everybody. Did I hear somebody mention Miz Lockwood? She's going to be here any minute now to give me my voice lesson on Buddy Boy's piano.

ETHYL. I'm surprised she's able to give a lesson at all after what happened this morning.

WANDA. You mean her piano getting broke?

ETHYL. I'm not talking about her piano. I'm talking about her *heart!*

WANDA. Her heart?

OLA BELLE. Miz Ethyl, you sure this isn't something you read in *True Story?*

ETHYL. *(outraged)* It most certainly is not! I saw it! Witnessed the whole thing!

FLORENE. Go ahead, Miz Ethyl. You've got our curiosity up now.

ETHYL. Well, I was over at Velma Bateman's this morning. And Velma's a next-door neighbor to that Miz

Lockwood. So, that band director feller she goes with—

WANDA. Mr. Bliss.

ETHYL. Yes. Whatever his name is. Anyway, he was over there. Velma says he's been there a right smart all summer. In fact — I guess I ought not to say this before Wanda, Florene — but Velma says sometimes his car is there all night.

HATTIE. I knew I ought not to let her touch Buddy Boy's piano.

WANDA. Miz Hattie, you promised!

FLORENE. Wanda, ssh! I want to hear this out.

ETHYL. Well, I was sitting there helping Velma shell peas when we heard 'em fussing and carrying on. She — the music teacher — kept saying, "You promised to marry me." And he kept saying she was a "g.d." liar, and he never done any such of a thing. He said he had *plans* for his life and didn't need her. That's when she started crying. Then she went to yelling, "What about *our* plans?" He said they never had any plans together. He had *his,* and now he was going out to take care of 'em. — Velma says he's got a real good job playing with some big orchestra somewhere. — So then she — this Miz Lockwood — took this horn that he plays—

WANDA. The cornet. He plays the cornet.

ETHYL. *(furious at the interruptions)* Well, whatever it was, she took it away from him and wasn't going to let him have it. See, that way she thought he couldn't go.

OLA BELLE. She should've just hit him right between the eyes with it.

FLORENE. Ola Belle! Sssh!

ETHYL. Well, he picked up a lamp, and he beat the tar out of her piano with it. Of course, that got her so upset that she let go of his horn, and when she did, he grabbed it and ran out the door and jumped in his car. So she dashed after him barefooted, begging him not to go, but he just backed on out into the street. Well, do you know that she chased him out onto that asphalt that was just as hot as fire and stood there in the street watching him drive off a hip-hoppin' her bare feet like she was doing a war dance and bawling for him to come back? The bottoms of her feet was blistered so bad until she couldn't even stand to put 'em on the ground, and Velma had to go out and help her get back in her house.

FLORENE. How awful!

ETHYL. Yes! She had to go to the doctor and get her feet bandaged up, and now she's on crutches. Pore thing! And doesn't even have a piano any more. And I guess he broke her lamp too. Isn't that sad?

OLA BELLE. Damned stupid if you ask me. What in the hell made her do that? It's women like her that give us all a bad name.

HATTIE. Ola Bella, cut out that cussin'. I won't have it on my porch.

WANDA. I don't believe it. Miz Lockwood wouldn't act that way.

FLORENE. It is surprising. Every time I've ever seen her she's acted like Miz Astor. I thought she had the world by the tail.

OLA BELLE. I wonder what the man's like that she made such a fool of herself over.

ETHYL. He looked kinda sissified to me. But Velma

said he sure can play pretty music. Said he had a pretty voice too. Her and him used to sing some together. No wonder she hated for him to leave. They must have had such a good time!

OLA BELLE. I think the law would have been on her side if she'd gone for the butcher knife when he tore up her piano.

HATTIE. Ola Belle's always looking for a excuse to kill one, ain't she? Well, I tell you, I think it serves her right for living in sin. Them blistered feet's just a foretaste of what's coming when she goes to hell.

WANDA. Shut up!

FLORENE. Wanda, who do you think you're talking to?

WANDA. Everybody. I want everybody to stop saying mean things about Miz Lockwood.

ETHYL. Oh, Honey, I didn't mean to be criticizing her. I just wish I'd ever met such an exciting man. I never knew one that was a bit of fun.

OLA BELLE. He sure sounds like a barrel of laughs.

WANDA. Shut your gossipin' old-lady mouths!

FLORENE. Wanda, you bridle your tongue right now, and apologize to everybody for being rude.

WANDA. No! I will not!

FLORENE. Wanda, you heard me.

WANDA. I won't say something just because you want me to. It *is* gossip, because Miz Lockwood wouldn't act that way. And I won't take back what I said.

*(ALTHEA appears at extreme USR on porch.)*

HATTIE. Well, we're fixin' to find out what's so. Here she comes.

ETHYL. Pore thing. she can barely walk. *(ALTHEA, who is on crutches and has both feet bandaged, drops her music.)* Oh, and she's dropped her music.

FLORENE. Wanda, go help her. *(WANDA does so.)*

OLA BELLE. He sure took the starch out of her collar, didn't he? *(WANDA and ALTHEA enter central porch area. ALTHEA is struggling along on her crutches. WANDA, looking mortified, carries her sheet music.)*

HATTIE. Howdee, Miz Lockwood.

ALTHEA. *(She looks up and realizes she is being watched by the four women. She attempts to muster some dignity.)* How do you do, ladies? I didn't realize Wanda was going to have a welcoming committee for me.

FLORENE. Hello, Miz Lockwood. We just got in from work and stopped here to get a little evening breeze.

ETHYL. Honey, I saw the whole thing from Velma Bateman's window. But don't you worry. I believe he'll be back. Who would want to run off and leave a pretty woman like you?

ALTHEA. I can't imagine what you're talking about, Miss Roberts, but I thank you for the compliment.

FLORENE. *(coming to her rescue)* It's nice of you to come over here to give Wanda her lesson, Miz Lockwood. I know she appreciates it.

ALTHEA. Well, we'd better hurry and get started, Wanda. We promised Mrs. Eaton we'd be finished in time for her supper.

WANDA. *(Still moritfied, she leads the way up the steps to HATTIE'S door.)* It's in here, Miz Lockwood.

HATTIE. You all be careful with that piano now.

ALTHEA. Don't you worry, Mrs. Eaton. I know how to take care of pianos. *(HATTIE, ETHYL, and OLA BELLE look at each other and titter. WANDA and ALTHEA enter HATTIE'S living room.)*

FLORENE. Imagine coming out to give a lesson after what happened to her!

ALTHEA. *(After she has disposed of her crutches and gotten settled on the piano bench.)* Let's run a few scales, Wanda, to warm up. *(She plays the scale WANDA will sing.)* Oh!

WANDA. What's wrong, Miz Lockwood?

ALTHEA. I'd better be careful using the pedals. I have to save my feet for the drive home. Let's go on. *(plays)*

WANDA.

DO, ME, SOL, DO, SOL, ME, DO
*(etc., finishing scale)*

ALTHEA. Very good, Wanda. Now what were you supposed to work on for today?

WANDA. "Young and Foolish" from *Plain and Fancy*.

ALTHEA. Oh, yes.

WANDA. But I don't know it very well yet. You said you'd sing it through to refresh me on the melody.

ALTHEA. *(stoically)* If that's what I said, then that's what I'll do. *(She plays and begins to sing in a highly trained voice.)*

YOUNG AND FOOLISH,
WHY IS IT WRONG TO BE
YOUNG AND FOOLISH?
WE HAVEN'T LONG TO BE.[18]
*(Her voice gathers emotion as she sings.)*
SOON ENOUGH THE CAREFREE DAYS,

THE SUNLIT DAYS GO BY.
SOON ENOUGH THE BLUEBIRD HAS TO FLY...19
*(breaking down)* I'm sorry, Wanda.

FLORENE. That was so pretty it made me cry.

OLA BELLE. She can really sing, can't she?

HATTIE. I reckon she's bawling over that band director feller. Can you beat that?

ETHYL. I think he'll come back. Don't you?

WANDA. Are you okay, Miz Lockwood?

ALTHEA. Yes, I'll be all right. That song just made me miss somebody.

WANDA. I don't see why you'd ever miss anybody, Miz Lockwood. If I was as pretty as you and could sing and play the piano, I never would be lonesome.

ALTHEA. I used to think that, Wanda. But I got more lonesome than I ever expected to.

WANDA. Miz Lockwood, did you hurt your feet like they say you did?

ALTHEA. How do they say I did it, Wanda?

WANDA. Miz Ethyl said you were running after Mr. Bliss to make him stay. But that's a lie, isn't it?

ALTHEA. No, Wanda. It's the truth. And here's the shocking part. I just wish I'd been able to stop him. I guess I'm a laughingstock, aren't I?

WANDA. I didn't laugh ... Miz Lockwood, see what bothers me is that I didn't think you would do something like that.

ALTHEA. I didn't either, Wanda. Isn't that funny? ... Well, we'd better hurry up and get through with your lesson so Mrs. Eaton won't miss her supper. What would you like to sing next, Wanda?

WANDA. *(dejected)* Nothing. I don't want to sing.

ALTHEA. Oh, Wanda, why don't we do one of those old songs that you like so much? *(thumbing through music)* Let's see. How about this? It's one of your best ones. *(She shows WANDA the one she has picked.)*

WANDA. *(without enthusiasm)* Oh, all right. *(ALTHEA plays and WANDA sings.)*

WHEN THE DEEP PURPLE FALLS
OVER SLEEPY GARDEN WALLS,[20]
*(The music becomes soft enough to permit the women on the porch to talk over it)*
AND THE STARS BEGIN TO FLICKER
IN THE SKY,[21]

FLORENE. *(Her dialogue overlapping the music.)* Oh, "Deep Purple"! I didn't know she was working on that. That's from my heyday. Remember, Ola Belle?

OLA BELLE. God, yes. I was so jealous of the way you sung. I thought you was going to set the world on fire.

FLORENE. So did I. *(She picks up the song, singing along softly with WANDA.)*

FLORENE and WANDA.
THRU THE MIST OF A MEMORY
YOU WANDER BACK TO ME,
BREATHING MY NAME
WITH A SIGH,[22]

ETHYL. Florene, get in there and sing with 'em.

FLORENE. Oh, no! I couldn't cut in on Wanda's lesson. She doesn't want to sing with me — or anything else.

ALTHEA. *(stops playing)* Who was that singing out there, Wanda?

WANDA. That was my mama.

ALTHEA. Well, what a beautiful voice she has! I see where you got your talent.

WANDA. Yes, ma'am. She taught me all those old songs. She was the first one in the family to have the idea of being a singer. But she never did anything about it.

ALTHEA. I see ... What a pity! At least she had the idea. That's a start. And she kept it alive for all these years. That made it a lot easier for you.

WANDA. I don't see how.

ALTHEA. You're an heiress, Wanda. You were born into singing. And now you must use your legacy ... We should go on before Mrs. Eaton runs us out. *(plays as WANDA sings)*

WANDA.

IN THE STILL OF THE NIGHT
ONCE AGAIN I HOLD YOU TIGHT,23
*(FLORENE joins in softly from porch.)*

FLORENE and WANDA.

THO' YOU'RE GONE,
YOUR LOVE LIVES ON
WHEN MOONLIGHT BEAMS,24

ETHYL. *(Runs up steps and calls through HATTIE'S screen door.)* Wanda, get your mama in there to sing with you.

FLORENE. Oh, no, Miz Ethyl!

ALTHEA. What do you say, Wanda?

WANDA. Well ... okay. *(Opens screen door and calls down to her mother.)* Mama, will you come help me finish this? *(ETHYL and OLA BELLE shove FLORENE inside to the piano and stand around to listen.)*

FLORENE. My goodness, I'm embarrassed! I just couldn't resist singing along.

ALTHEA. Come on, Florene. I know you know it. We'll pick up here. *(Indicating where they are on music. She plays.)*

FLORENE and WANDA. *(singing together)*
AND AS LONG AS MY HEART WILL BEAT,
LOVER, WE'LL ALWAYS MEET
HERE IN MY DEEP PURPLE DREAMS.25
*(ETHYL and OLA BELLE applaud when it is over.)*

FLORENE. Miz Lockwood, I—

ALTHEA. "Althea," Florene — please.

FLORENE. All right. Althea, I want to thank you for ... for letting me sing "Deep Purple." It's the first time I ever got to do it with a piano.

OLA BELLE. I had forgot just how good you sing, Florene. I'm still jealous.

ALTHEA. Let's do one we all know so nobody has to be left out. Where's Mrs. Eaton? She ought to be in on this too.

ETHYL. *(Runs out door and part of the way down steps.)* Hattie, get in here. You're missing out on all the fun. We're about to do one together.

HATTIE. *(still in glider)* I can't sing. Never could. Neither can you, Ethyl, for that matter.

ETHYL. *(Undaunted, she races back up steps and into HATTIE'S living room.)* What about hymns? You and Buddy Boy used to do plenty of them on this very piano. Where's that old hymnal she had? *(scratches through papers on piano)* Here it is. Do "Unclouded Day," Miz Lockwood. We all know that. *(FLORENE, WANDA, and ETHYL gather around ALTHEA at piano. OLA BELLE hangs back toward the door.)*

ALTHEA. Ola Belle, will you sit here on the bench with me and work these pedals?

OLA BELLE. *(moving to piano bench)* Well, I can sure move my feet even if I can't sing.

FLORENE. Wanda, you sing soprano, and I'll take the alto part.

ALTHEA. Is everybody ready? *(plays)*

EVERYBODY.

O THEY TELL ME OF A HOME
FAR BEYOND THE SKIES,
O THEY TELL ME OF A HOME FAR AWAY;26
*(HATTIE rises and starts up steps.)*
O THEY TELL ME OF A HOME
WHERE NO STORM CLOUDS RISE,
O THEY TELL ME OF AN UNCLOUDED DAY.27

HATTIE. *(entering her living room)* Ya'll nearly drug that verse to death.

FLORENE. Well then, you better get in here and show us how to do it, Miz Hattie.

HATTIE. Be careful, Ola Belle. I don't want you ruining my piano with your big feet.

OLA BELLE. Yes, ma'am.

ALTHEA. We'll start from the chorus. And pick it up this time.

*(As she plays, thunder is heard in the distance.)*

EVERYBODY.
O THE LAND OF CLOUDLESS DAY,

O THE LAND OF AN UNCLOUDED DAY;
O THEY TELL ME OF A HOME WHERE NO
  STORM CLOUDS RISE,
O THEY TELL ME OF AN UNCLOUDED DAY.28

*(Just as they finish, there is more thunder.)*

OLA BELLE. Doesn't sound like we're going to have a cloudless day.

HATTIE. Naw, I seen some little thunderheads over in the west.

OLA BELLE. Well, shit! Excuse me. I hope the roads won't be slick when we have to drive to work tomorrow.

ETHYL. A rain would cool things off.

HATTIE. It'll be good for that little pecan tree I planted this afternoon.

*(More distant thunder is heard.)*

FLORENE. Well, rain or no rain, I'm driving us to work tomorrow, Ola Belle. And I'm going to pass anything that gets in my way.

OLA BELLE. Uh-oh. We better look out now.

FLORENE. We've interrupted your lesson, Wanda. I'm sorry.

WANDA. That's okay. It was fun to sing together.

ALTHEA. You still have some time, Wanda. If Mrs. Eaton doesn't mind, why don't I play one more song for you to do by yourself?

OLA BELLE. Sing something pretty for us, Sug.

WANDA. Well, okay. I'll do this one — the one I sang in the contest, Mama. I still like it, even if I didn't win.

FLORENE. Go on, Wanda. You have the stage. *(WANDA hands the music to ALTHEA, who plays as WANDA sings.)*

WANDA.
GOLDEN DAYS IN THE SUNSHINE OF OUR
  HAPPY YOUTH,
GOLDEN DAYS FULL OF INNOCENCE AND
  FULL OF TRUTH!
IN OUR HEARTS WE REMEMBER THEM ALL
  ELSE ABOVE,
GOLDEN DAYS, DAYS OF YOUTH AND LOVE![29]

*(Lights fade to black. End of Act II.)*

# PROPERTY PLOT

## ACT I, SCENE 1

*Kings' side:*
Sofa (SC)
Coffee table (in front of sofa)
on:
> *Life* Magazine, open
> *Photoplay* Magazines
> Tablet and pencil

End table (SR of sofa)
on:
> Lamp

Easy chair (SR of end table)
Console radio (US of sofa)
Three-drawer dresser with mirror (SL)
on:
> Lipstick, rouge, powder, etc.
> Comb and brush
> Jewelry box
> in:
>> Earrings
>> Necklace
>
> Perfume
> Framed photo of Killer King (turned away from audience)
> Two trophies
> One bottle red nail polish
> Box of tissues
> Cold cream
> Bobby pins
> Nail file
> Compact mirror

*(All dresser drawers are full of clothes.)*

# THE ALTO PART

**Closet (SL wall US of dresser)**
in:
    On shelf:
      Ouija board and planchette
    Hanging:
      Women's clothes, including Florene's sundress
      Girl's clothes, including schooldresses for Wanda
    On floor:
      Florene's sandals
      Wanda's houseshoes

*Hattie's side:*
**Piano (USR)**
on:
    Hattie's purse
    Framed photo of Buddy Boy
**Table (SL)**
on:
    Telephone
    Bible
**Console tetevision (USL)**
on:
    Rabbit ears
    Clock
**Rocking chair (DSL)**
**Curtains (on foyer windows) closed**

*Porch:*
**Glider (USC)**
**Wicker chair (SL of glider)**
**Bench (DSR)**

# THE ALTO PART

*Personal props:*
Baptist Standard (Wanda)
Large painting (Ethyl)

## ACT I, SCENE 2

*Kings' side:*
Same as I, 1 but add:
On coffee table:
    Envelope
    Newspaper
    Tray with:
        Pitcher of iced tea
        Two glasses
On dresser:
    Empty change purse
On sofa:
    Folded, ironed clothes
On closet door:
    Women's ironed clothes on hangers
Ironing board (DSL) with:
    Iron
    Iron stand
    Sprinkler bottle

*Personal props:*
Schoolbooks (Wanda)
Lunchbox (Wanda)
Change purse with $2.50 (Althea)
Six-pack of beer (Ola Belle)
Bottle opener (Ola Belle)

*(Strike tray with pitcher of tea and glasses, schoolbooks, lunch kit, ironing board, iron, iron stand, sprinkler bottle, newspaper, envelope, change purse.)*

## ACT I, SCENE 3

*Kings' side:*
Same as before but add:
On sofa:
    Pillow
    Blanket
On coffee table:
    Letter
On end table:
    Florene's purse
    Paper lunch bag
Small suitcase (on floor in front of dresser) in:
    Folded clothes
    Map

*Personal props:*
Clothes to pack (Florene)
Toiletries to pack (Florene)
Duster (Wanda)
Toast (Wanda)
Overnight bag (Ola Belle)
Purse (Ola Belle)
in:
    $2.00

*(Strike pillow, blanket, and overnight bag.)*

## ACT II, SCENE 1

*Kings' side:*
Dresser top is restored to same as I, 1

Add:
On dresser:
    1 bottle red nail polish
On radio:
    Flyswatter
    Envelope of sheet music
On coffee table:
    *Photoplay* Magazine, open
In closet:
    Hanging:
        Florene's rose linen dress from I, 1
On floor:
    Florene's white pumps from I, 1

*Hattie's side:*
Same as before but add:
On piano:
    Paper fan
On telephone table:
    Bible

*Personal props:*
Change purse (Florene)
Pecan pie (Hattie)
Knife (Florene)
Napkins (Florene)
Pills (Florene)
Glass of water (Florene)

*(Strike from Kings' side: pie, napkins, and knife. Restore dresser to same as I, 1. Strike from Hattie's side: pills, water glass, and paper fan.)*

## ACT II, SCENE 2

*Porch:*
Same as before

*Personal props:*
Paper fan (Florene)
Handkerchief (Florene)

## ACT II, SCENE 3

*Kings' side:*
Same as before but add:
On sofa:
    Pillow and blanket
On end table:
    Florene's purse
    in:
        Wallet
On coffee table:
    Recipe
On radio:
    Envelope of sheet music

*Personal props:*
Two suitcases (Wanda)—one is from I, 3
Stockings (Wanda)
Dress and shoes from I, 1 (Wanda)

*(Strike suitcases, note on door, pillow, and blanket. Restore dresser top, except strike photo of Killer King and trophies.)*

## ACT II, SCENE 4

*Kings' side:*
Same as before
On radio:
    Envelope of sheet music

*Hattie's side:*
Same as before but add:
On piano:
    Hymnal

*Porch:*
Same as before

*Personal props:*
Sunbonnet (Hattie)
Dust rag (Wanda)
Crutches (Althea)
Bandages (on feet) (Althea)
Sheet music (Althea)

# **COSTUME PLOT**

## ACT I, SCENE 1

FLORENE:
- Rose linen dress
- White pumps
- Stockings
- Garter belt
- Slip
- Necklace
- Earrings

*

- Print sundress
- Sandals

WANDA:
- White, organdy lace dress with pink sash
- Women's stockings
- White sandals

HATTIE:
- Navy and white print dress
- Black shoes
- Brooch
- Stockings
- Purse

OLA BELLE:
- White uniform
- White oxfords
- White stockings
- Purse

# THE ALTO PART

ETHYL:
>Print dress
>Pumps
>Necklace
>Earrings

## ACT I, SCENE 2

FLORENE:
>Print sundress (from I, 1)
>Sandals
>Apron

ETHYL:
>Print dress (from I, 1)
>Pumps
>Smock

WANDA:
>Plaid school dress
>Loafers
>Socks

ALTHEA:
>Apricot taffeta dress with bolero
>White pumps
>Stockings
>Change purse

OLA BELLE:
>White uniform
>White oxfords

# THE ALTO PART

White stockings
Purse

## ACT I, SCENE 3

**FLORENE:**
Red sleeveless dress
White pumps
Earrings
Necklace
Purse

**WANDA:**
Nightgown
Duster
Houseshoes

**OLA BELLE:**
White uniform
Houseshoes
Purse

## ACT II, SCENE 1

**OLA BELLE:**
Beige skirt
Plaid blouse
Flats
Purse

**WANDA:**
White shorts
Blue blouse

# THE ALTO PART

    Loafers

FLORENE:
    Green circle skirt
    Yellow, cap-sleeved blouse
    Sandals
    Change purse

HATTIE:
    Light blue print dress
    Apron
    White sandals
    Stockings

\*

    Blue, long-sleeved robe
ETHYL:
    Pastel dress with bolero
    Pink hat with tassel
    Pumps
    Earrings
    Gloves

## ACT II, SCENE 2

HATTIE:
    Light blue print dress (from II, 1)
    White sandals
    Stockings

FLORENE:
    Black crepe dress
    Black pillbox hat

Black pumps
Black gloves
Black purse

## ACT II, SCENE 3

**HATTIE:**
Blue robe (from II, 1)

**FLORENE:**
Flowered robe

*

Slip
Stockings
Rose linen dress (from I, 1)

**WANDA:**
Nightgown

*

White, organdy lace dress with pink sash (from I, 1)
White sandals

## ACT II, SCENE 4

**WANDA:**
White shorts (from II, 1)
Plaid shirt
Loafers

**HATTIE:**
Brown print dress
White sandals
Stockings

Sunbonnet

**FLORENE:**
White uniform
White oxfords
White stockings
Purse

**OLA BELLE:**
White uniform
White stockings
White oxfords
Purse

**ETHYL:**
Pastel dress (from II, 1) without bolero
Pumps

**ALTHEA:**
Gold princess-style dress
White sandals (on bandaged feet)

# FOOTNOTES

PAGE

9    1 "Garden of the Moon" by Harry Warren, Al Dubin and Johnny Mercer, Copyright 1938 by Warner Bros. Inc., Copyright Renewed, Used By Permission, All Rights Reserved.

9    2 *Ibid.*

10    3 *Ibid.*

17    4 *Ibid.*

29    5 "Maybe" Words by Allan Flynn, Music by Franklin Madden, Copyright 1935. Renewed 1963 by Robbins Music Corporation. All rights assigned to CBS CATALOGUE PARTNERSHIP. All rights administered and controlled by CBS Robbins Catalog, Inc. International Copyright Secured. All Rights Reserved.

29    6 *Ibid.*

29    7 *Ibid.*

29    8 *Ibid.*

45    9 "It's Only A Paper Moon" by Harold Arlen, E.Y. Harburg and Billy Rose, Copyright 1933 by Ann-Rachel Music Corp. and Warner Bros. Music, Copyright Renewed, Assigned to Chappell and Co., Inc., (Intersong-USA, Inc., Publisher) and Warner Bros. Music, Used By Permission, All Rights Reserved.

## FOOTNOTES
*(continued)*

45    10 *Ibid.*

45    11 *Ibid.*

45    12 *Ibid.*

45    13 *Ibid.*

46    14 *Ibid.*

75    15 "Maybe," previously cited.

76    16 *Ibid.*

81    17 *Ibid.*

97    18 "Young and Foolish" by A.B. Horwitt and Albert Hague, Copyright 1954 by Chappell and Co., Inc., Copyright Renewed, Used By Permission, All Rights Reserved.

98    19 *Ibid.*

99    20 "Deep Purple" Words by Mitchell Parish, Music by Peter DeRose. Copyright 1934, 1939. Copyright Renewed 1962, 1967, by Robbins Music Corporation. All rights assigned to CBS CATALOGUE PARTNERSHIP. All rights administered and controlled by CBS Robbins Catalog, Inc. International Copyright Secured. All Rights Reserved.

## FOOTNOTES
*(continued)*

99     21 *Ibid.*

99     22 *Ibid.*

100    23 *Ibid.*

100    24 *Ibid.*

101    25 *Ibid.*

102    26 "The Unclouded Day" by Rev. J. K. Alwood *(Public Domain)*

102    27 *Ibid.*

103    28 *Ibid.*

104    29 "Golden Days" by Sigmund Romberg and Dorothy Donnelly, Copyright 1924 by Warner Bros. Inc., Copyright Renewed, Used By Permission, All Rights Reserved.

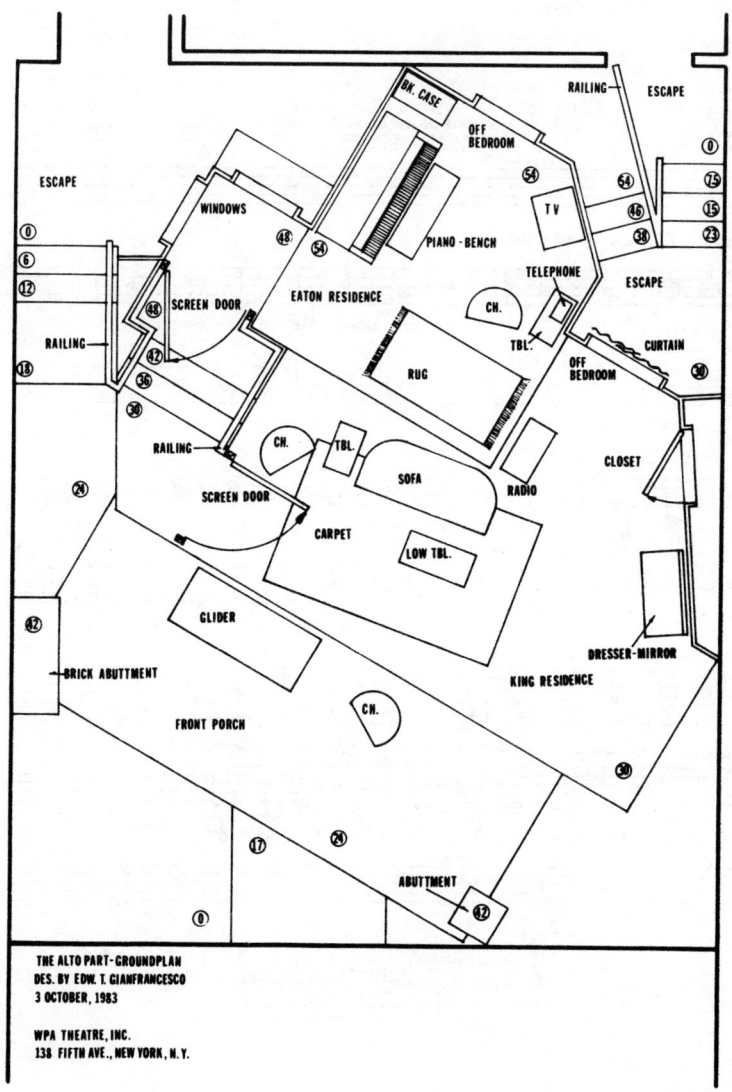

# MAYBE

Bluebird Record No. B10793

by
ALLAN FLYNN
FRANK MADDEN

Copyright 1935 Robbins Music Corporation, 799 Seventh Avenue, New York, N.Y.
International Copyright secured.                     Made in U.S.A.

All Rights Reserved Including Public Performance For Profit.
Any arrangement or adaptation of this composition without the consent of the owner is an infringement of copyright

# DEEP PURPLE

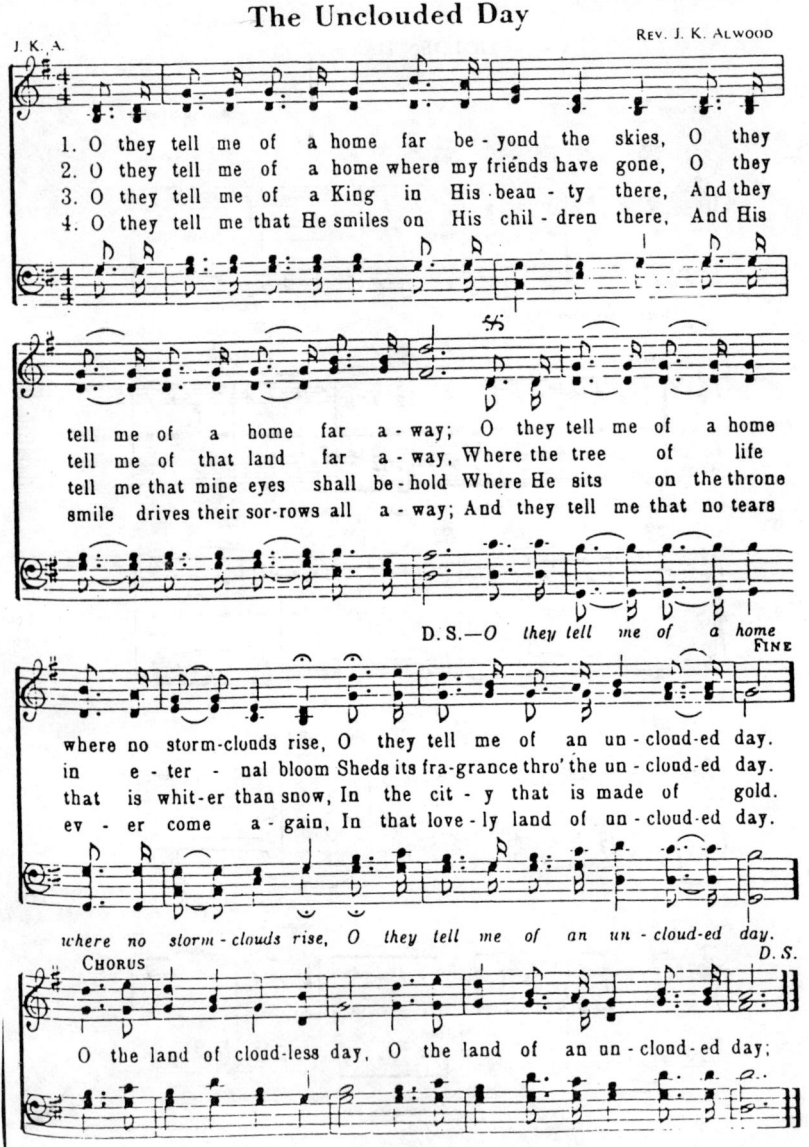